Hiring Your Boss

Mastering Clarity, Positioning, and Alignment to Land Your Dream Job

Obrian Kerr

Table of Contents

Introduction

Ever feel like the job search is a one-sided game, where you're endlessly pitching yourself to companies, hoping they'll deem you worthy? It's exhausting, demoralizing, and frankly, outdated.

The truth is, you have more power than you think.

In this book, I'm going to show you how to flip the script. You're not just looking for a job; you're hiring your boss. Yes, you read that right. You're the one calling the shots, evaluating the company, the culture, and most importantly, the person you'll be reporting to.

Welcome to the "Hire Your Boss" Revolution

This isn't just a clever turn of phrase; it's a mindset shift, a radical rethinking of the job search process. It's about taking control, defining your terms, and ultimately, finding a workplace that aligns with your values, goals, and aspirations.

Imagine walking into an interview not as a nervous applicant, but as a discerning professional assessing whether this company is the right fit for you. Imagine negotiating your salary and benefits not as a desperate plea, but as a confident discussion about what you bring to the table. Imagine starting a new job not with dread, but with excitement and anticipation.

That's the power of hiring your boss.

The Blueprint: Clarity, Positioning, and

Alignment

But how do you actually hire your boss? It's not as complicated as it sounds. In fact, it all boils down to three simple, yet powerful, principles:

1.   **Clarity:** Get crystal clear about what you want in a job, a company, and a boss. This means digging deep into your values, your passions, and your long-term career goals.

2.   **Positioning:** Brand yourself as the ideal candidate for your dream job. This means showcasing your unique skills and experiences, highlighting your accomplishments, and building a strong professional network.

3.   **Alignment:** Find a company and a boss whose values and vision align with yours. This means doing your research, asking the right questions, and trusting your gut.

Think of these three principles as your personal compass, guiding you through the job search process with confidence and clarity.

Why This Book Is Different

You might be thinking, "Okay, this sounds interesting, but how is this book different from all the other career advice out there?"

I'm glad you asked. Here's why:

•   **Practical Strategies:** This book isn't filled with fluffy platitudes or vague advice. I provide actionable strategies, step-by-step guides, and real-world examples to help you implement the "Hire Your Boss" framework.

• **Relatable Stories:** You'll hear inspiring stories from real people who have successfully "hired their boss." Their experiences will motivate you and show you that anything is possible.

• **Proven Results:** The "Hire Your Boss" method has been tested and proven to work. I've seen it transform countlesscareers, and I know it can do the same for you.

Who This Book Is For

This book is for anyone who's tired of the traditional job search. It's for recent graduates, mid-career professionals, career changers, and anyone who wants to take control of their career destiny.

It doesn't matter what your background is or what industry you're in. If you're ready to stop settling for less and start demanding more from your career, this book is for you.

Your Journey Begins Here

Over the next few chapters, we'll delve deep into each of the three principles – Clarity, Positioning, and Alignment. You'll learn how to:

• Uncover your hidden passions and talents

• Create a compelling personal brand that sets you apart

• Network like a pro and build meaningful

relationships

- Master the art of interviewing and salary negotiation

Find companies whose values align with your own and that's just the beginning.

By the end of this book, you'll have the tools and the mindset to confidently hire your boss and land the job of your dreams.

So, are you ready to take charge of your career? Are you ready to stop playing by someone else's rules and start defining your own success?

If so, let's get started. Your journey begins here.

A Glimpse of What's Ahead

To give you a taste of what's to come, here's a sneak peek at someof the stories and insights you'll find in this book:

- The self-taught coder who landed a job at a top tech company by showcasing his skills and passion.

- The medical assistant who transitioned into a management role by leveraging her experience and pursuing additional certifications.

- The sales professional who doubled her salary by clearly articulating her value proposition and negotiating confidently.

- And many more...

These stories are a testament to the power of the "Hire

Your Boss" mindset. They show that anyone can achieve their career goals with the right strategies and a bit of determination.

Your Turn

I'm excited to embark on this journey with you. Together, we'll rewrite the rules of the job search and empower you to hire your boss.

Are you ready to take the first step? Let's dive in!

Part I: Laying the Foundation

Chapter 1: The Job Market Reimagined

Forget everything you think you know about the job market. The old rules no longer apply.

The days of sending out hundreds of resumes and hoping for a response are over. The days of groveling for an interview and accepting whatever offer comes your way are long gone.

The job market has changed, and it's time to change with it.

A Landscape in Flux

The traditional job market was a battlefield. Companies held all the cards, and job seekers were forced to scramble for scraps.

But something remarkable has happened. The power dynamics are shifting.

With the rise of remote work, the war for talent, and the changing priorities of the younger generations, companies are realizing that they need to adapt to attract and retain top talent.

This means you, the job seeker, have more leverage than ever before. You are not just a cog in the machine; you are a valuable asset. And it's time you started acting like it.

From Applicant to Asset

The "Hire Your Boss" mindset is about recognizing your

worth and refusing to settle for anything less than a job that fulfills you both professionally and personally.

It's about understanding that you are not simply an applicant; you are a potential asset to any company you choose to join.

You bring skills, experience, and a unique perspective that can help a company grow and thrive. And that's something worth celebrating.

A New Set of Rules

In this chapter, we're going to tear down the old rules of the job market and rewrite them in your favor.

You'll learn:

How to leverage the current trends: We'll explore the factors that are shaping the job market today and how you can use them to your advantage.

How to embrace a proactive mindset: It's time to stop waiting for opportunities to come to you and start actively creating them.

How to position yourself as an asset: You'll learn how to showcase your unique skills and experiences to attract the right opportunities.

By the end of this chapter, you'll have a fresh perspective on the job market and a renewed sense of empowerment. You'll understand that you are not just a job seeker; you are a force to be reckoned with.

So, are you ready to reimagine the job market and unleash your full potential?

Let's dive in!

The Power Shift

The job market isn't what it used to be. It's a dynamic, ever-changing landscape where the old rules no longer apply. The days of simply sending out resumes and waiting for the phone to ring are long gone.

Today's job market is a complex ecosystem, influenced by technological advancements, shifting economic trends, and a globalized workforce. The rise of automation and artificial intelligence is reshaping industries, creating new roles while rendering others obsolete. The gig economy is on the rise, offering flexible work arrangements but also increased competition.

In this shifting landscape, job seekers need to be more than just qualified; they need to be proactive, adaptable, and strategic. The "post and pray" approach won't cut it anymore. You need to take charge of your career destiny and position yourself as the candidate companies can't afford to pass up.

A New Era of Empowerment

While this may sound daunting, it's actually an exciting time to be a job seeker. The power is shifting from employers to employees. Companies are no longer just interviewing you; you're interviewing them. You have the opportunity to assess whether their culture, values, and mission align with your own. You can demand more than just a paycheck; you can seek out opportunities for growth, development, and fulfillment.

But to seize this power, you need to be proactive. You need to understand the changing job landscape, identify your unique strengths and values, and proactively seek out opportunities that align with your career goals.

According to a recent study by the World Economic Forum, "65% of children entering primary school today will ultimately end up working in completely new job types that don't yet exist."This means that the skills and knowledge you acquire today may notbe relevant in the future. To stay competitive, you need to be a lifelong learner, constantly updating your skillset and adapting to new technologies and trends.

The Proactive Job Seeker

So, what does it mean to be a proactive job seeker? It means:

Continuously learning and growing: Invest in your professional development by taking courses, attending workshops, and reading industry publications.

Building a strong personal brand: Craft a compelling online presence that showcases your skills, experience, and personality.

Networking strategically: Build relationships with people in your field and attend industry events to stay informed and connected.

Tailoring your applications: Customize your resume and cover letter for each job you apply to, highlighting your relevant skills and experience.

Preparing for interviews: Research the company, practice answering common questions, and be ready to articulate your value proposition.

Negotiating confidently: Know your worth and don't be afraid to ask for what you deserve.

By taking a proactive approach to your job search, you'll not only increase your chances of landing your dream job but also set yourself up for long-term career success. The job market may be changing, but with the right mindset and strategies, you can thrive.

You're in the Driver's Seat

It's easy to feel powerless in the job market. You send out countless resumes, tailor cover letters to perfection, and eagerly await responses that often never come. It can feel like you're at the mercy of faceless hiring managers, your fate hanging on a single email or phone call. But this is a misconception.

The reality is, job seekers wield far more influence than they realize. You possess a unique set of skills, experiences, and perspectives that companies desperately need. You're not simply a replaceable cog in the machine; you're a potential asset, a valuable contributor who can drive innovation and growth.

Shifting the Power Dynamic

The traditional job search model is inherently imbalanced. Job seekers are often seen as supplicants, pleading for a chance to prove their worth. This outdated approach not only diminishes your power but also prevents you from finding a truly fulfilling career.

To hire your boss, you must first recognize your own value. You are not just another applicant; you are a skilled professional with a distinct set of talents and aspirations. By embracing this mindset shift, you reclaim your agency and transform the job search from a passive endeavor to an active pursuit.

Your Skills Are in Demand

In today's rapidly evolving economy, companies are constantly seeking individuals with specialized skills and fresh perspectives. Whether you're a seasoned professional or a recent graduate, your expertise is valuable. The key is to identify your unique strengths and effectively communicate them to potential employers.

As renowned career coach Richard N. Bolles writes in his classic book *What Color Is Your Parachute?*, "The skills you've already used in paid jobs, or in volunteer work, or in your hobbies at home, are very likely to be exactly the skills you'll need and want to use in your next job." (Bolles 2023, 67) By recognizing and leveraging your existing skills, you position yourself as a sought-after candidate.

You Have the Power of Choice

One of the most empowering aspects of hiring your boss is the ability to choose where you work. You're not limited to accepting any job offer that comes your way. Instead, you can carefully evaluate each opportunity based on your criteria and select the one that best aligns with your goals and values.

As bestselling author Ramit Sethi advises in his book *I Will Teach You to Be Rich*, "Don't just take the first job that comes along. Be picky. Find a company that excites you, a boss you can learn from, and a role that challenges you." (Sethi 2019, 145) By exercising your power of choice, you ensure that your career trajectory is one that you consciously design.

You Can Shape Your Compensation

Salary negotiation is often a daunting prospect for job seekers. Many feel uncomfortable discussing money or fear jeopardizing an offer by asking for more. However, negotiating your compensation is an essential part of hiring your boss.

According to Linda Babcock and Sara Laschever's groundbreaking book *Women Don't Ask*, failing to negotiate can have significant long-term consequences for your earning potential. (Babcock and Laschever 2007, 34) By approaching negotiation with confidence and preparation, you can secure a compensation package that reflects your worth.

Building Your Brand

In the digital age, personal branding is more important than ever. Your online presence, including your LinkedIn profile, personal website, and social media activity, can significantly impact your job prospects. By strategically crafting your personal brand, you showcase your expertise and attract opportunities that align with your career goals.

William Arruda, a leading personal branding expert, emphasizes the importance of authenticity in his book *Ditch. Dare. Do!*, stating, "Your personal brand is not about creating a façade; it's about revealing your best self." (Arruda 2015, 48) By sharing your unique story and expertise online, you connect with potential employers on a deeper level and stand out from the crowd.

The "Hire Your Boss" Mindset in Action

To truly harness the power of hiring your boss, you must adopt a proactive and confident approach to the job search. This means:

Setting Clear Goals: Define your ideal job, company

culture, and boss.

Networking Strategically: Build relationships with industryprofessionals and learn about potential opportunities.

Preparing Thoroughly for Interviews: Research the company, practice your responses, and showcase your value proposition.

Negotiating Assertively: Know your worth and advocate for your desired compensation.

Following Up Persistently: Maintain communication withpotential employers and express your continued interest.

By embracing these strategies, you transform the job search from a passive waiting game into an active pursuit of your ideal career. You're not just looking for a job; you're hiring your boss.

From Reactive to Strategic

Let's face it: the conventional job search often feels like a frantic chase, a relentless pursuit of elusive opportunities. You tirelessly scroll through endless job boards, fire off generic resumes and cover letters into the void, and anxiously await responses that rarely come. If you're lucky enough to snag an interview, you find yourself nervously trying to impress a panel of strangers, hoping they'll see your potential.

This reactive approach leaves you feeling powerless, at the mercy of faceless recruiters and unpredictable algorithms. It's a soul-sucking cycle that can leave even the most qualified candidates feeling defeated and demoralized.

But what if there was a better way?

Enter the "Hire Your Boss" Mindset

The "Hire Your Boss" philosophy is your escape route from this hamster wheel of frustration. It's a radical shift in perspective that empowers you to take control of your career destiny. Instead of chasing after jobs, you become a magnet, attracting opportunities that align with your unique talents and aspirations.

The Paradigm Shift

This shift involves a fundamental change in your approach:

From Applicant to Assessor: You're not just an applicant; you're an assessor, evaluating whether a company and a boss are the right fit for you.

From Pleading to Partnering: You're not begging for a job; you're proposing a partnership, showcasing how your skills and experience can contribute to the company's success.

From Reactive to Proactive: You're not waiting for opportunities to come to you; you're actively seeking out companies that align with your values and goals.

The Strategic Advantage

By adopting this strategic mindset, you gain several key advantages:

Confidence: You approach the job search with a sense of self-assuredness, knowing you're not just a job seeker but a valuable asset.

Clarity: You focus your efforts on opportunities that truly resonate with you, avoiding the time-wasting pursuit of misaligned roles.

Authenticity: You present your true self, showcasing your unique strengths and personality, which attracts employerswho value what you bring to the table.

Results: You're more likely to land a job that you love, where you can thrive and make a meaningful impact.

From Theory to Practice

So, how do you make this shift from reactive to strategic? Here aresome practical steps:

Define Your Ideal Job: Get crystal clear about the type of role, company culture, and boss you want to work for. (See Chapter 2 for guidance on clarifying your career vision.)

Build Your Personal Brand: Craft a compelling personal brand that showcases your unique skills and experiences. (See Chapter 4 for tips on positioning yourself as the ideal candidate.)

Network Intentionally: Focus on building genuine relationships with people in your field, rather than just collecting business cards. (See Chapter 7 for strategies on networking with purpose.)

Target Your Search: Research companies that align with your values and goals, and tailor your applications accordingly. (See Chapter 6 for guidance on finding the right cultural fit.)

Ace the Interview: Approach interviews as a two-way conversation, where you're assessing the company as much as they're assessing you. (See Chapter 8 for tips on mastering the interview process.)

The "Hire Your Boss" Difference

The "Hire Your Boss" approach isn't just about landing a job; it's about finding a fulfilling career path that aligns with your passions and purpose. It's about taking ownership of your professional destiny and creating a future that excites and inspires you.

As Bolles (2017) puts it, "The job-hunt is not about finding a job; it is about creating a life that you can love." By embracing the "Hire Your Boss" mindset, you're not just seeking employment; you're embarking on a transformative journey towards a more meaningful and rewarding career.

Chapter 2: Clarity: Your North Star

Imagine setting off on a cross-country road trip without a map, GPS, or even a destination in mind. You might enjoy the scenery for a while, but eventually, you'll end up lost, frustrated, andwondering why you even started this journey in the first place.

That's what the job search feels like for many people: a meandering path with no clear direction. You apply to dozens of jobs, hoping one will stick, but you're not really sure what you're looking for.

It's time to change that.

In this chapter, we're going to ditch the aimless wandering and equip you with a powerful navigation tool: Clarity. Think of it as your personal North Star, guiding you through the job search process with unwavering focus and purpose.

Clarity is about more than just knowing what kind of job you want. It's about understanding your values, your passions, and your long-term career aspirations. It's about defining what success means to you, both personally and professionally.

Why is clarity so important? Because it allows you to:

• **Target your search:** Instead of applying to any job that seems remotely interesting, you'll be able to focus your efforts on opportunities that truly align with your goals.

• **Craft a compelling narrative:** When you know what you want, you can communicate it clearly and confidently to potential employers.

• **Make informed decisions:** With a clear vision in mind, you'll be able to evaluate job offers based on how well they fit your overall career plan.

• **Stay motivated:** When you're working towards a goal that truly matters to you, you'll be more resilient in the face of setbacks and rejection.

In short, clarity is the foundation of a successful job search. Without it, you're essentially shooting in the dark, hoping to hit the target by chance.

But with clarity, you can take aim and hit the bullseye.

In the following sections, we'll dive deep into the concept of clarity. We'll explore different tools and techniques for uncovering your passions, defining your values, and creating a crystal-clear vision for your career.

By the end of this chapter, you'll have a roadmap that will guide you towards your dream job with confidence and purpose. You'll no longer be a passive job seeker, but a proactive career architect, building a future that excites and fulfills you.

So, are you ready to find your North Star? Let's get started.

Defining Clarity

Picture this: You're lost in a dense forest, with no map, no compass, and no sense of direction. You wander aimlessly, hopingto stumble upon a way out, but the more you walk, the more disoriented you become. That's what the job search can feel like without clarity.

Clarity is your compass in the job search wilderness. It's the guiding principle that helps you navigate the twists and turns of the hiring process, leading you towards your desired destination—the job of your dreams.

What is Clarity?

In the context of your career, clarity is the deep understanding of what you truly want from your professional life. It's about knowing your values, your passions, your strengths, and your ideal work environment. It's about having a crystal-clear vision of your career path and the steps you need to take to get there.

Why Clarity is Crucial

Without clarity, your job search is like shooting arrows in the dark. You might hit a target eventually, but it's unlikely to be the bullseye. You might land a job, but it might not be the right job foryou.

Here's why clarity is essential in the job search journey:

• **Focused Job Search:** When you know what you want, you can target your search efforts more effectively. You won't waste time applying for jobs that don't align with your goals or values.

- **Compelling Personal Brand:** Clarity allows you to articulate your unique value proposition with confidence. You can tailor your resume, cover letters, and LinkedIn profile to showcase the skills and experiences that matter most to your target employers.

- **Strategic Networking:** With clarity, you can network with intention, focusing on building relationships with people who can help you achieve your career goals.

- **Confident Interviews:** When you know what you bring to the table, you can confidently answer interview questions and showcase your strengths.

- **Successful Negotiations:** Clarity gives you the leverage to negotiate a compensation package that reflects your worth and aligns with your career aspirations.

In short, clarity is the foundation upon which your entire job search is built. It's the key to attracting the right opportunities and landing the job that truly fulfills you.

The Fog of Uncertainty

If you're feeling lost or unsure about your career direction, you're not alone. According to a 2018 Gallup poll, only 33% of American workers feel engaged at work. This means that the majority of people are going through the motions, feeling unfulfilled and uninspired. (Gallup, 2018).

The lack of clarity is a major contributor to this widespread disengagement. When people don't know what they want from their careers, it's easy to fall into a rut, feeling trapped and unmotivated.

The Path to Clarity

The good news is that clarity is not something you're born with. It's something you can develop and cultivate over time. Here are a few strategies to help you gain clarity:

• **Self-Reflection:** Take some time to reflect on your values, passions, strengths, and weaknesses. What do you enjoy doing? What are you good at? What kind of work environment do you thrive in?

• **Explore Your Options:** Research different career paths and industries that interest you. Talk to people who are working in those fields to get an inside perspective.

• **Seek Guidance:** Consider working with a career coach or mentor who can help you clarify your goals and develop a plan of action.

• **Experiment:** Try out different jobs or volunteer opportunities to gain hands-on experience and see what you enjoy.

The Power of a Career Vision

Once you have a clearer understanding of your career goals, it's time to create a career vision. This is a vivid and compelling picture of your ideal future, including your desired job title, industry, company culture, and lifestyle.

Your career vision is like a roadmap that guides your decisions and actions. It helps you stay focused and motivated, even when facedwith challenges or setbacks.

In the next section, we'll delve deeper into the process of creating a powerful career vision. But for now, start by reflecting on the questions below to gain clarity on your career aspirations:

- What are my core values?

- What am I passionate about?

- What are my unique strengths and skills?

- What kind of work environment do I thrive in?

- What impact do I want to make in the world?

By taking the time to answer these questions honestly and thoughtfully, you'll be well on your way to achieving clarity and unlocking your full career potential.

Uncovering Your Passions

Let's face it: most of us don't wake up knowing exactly what we want to do with our lives. Passion isn't always a lightning bolt of inspiration; sometimes, it's a slow burn, a quiet whisper that needs to be unearthed.

This section is your archaeological dig, your journey to uncover the career gold buried within you. We'll delve into exercises and reflections designed to illuminate your passions, strengths, and values – the trifecta that will guide you towards a career that not only pays the bills but also ignites your soul.

Why Passions Matter (And How to Find Yours)

Passion isn't just about loving what you do; it's the fuel that propels you forward, the spark that keeps you engaged and motivated even when faced with challenges. When you're passionate about your work, you're more likely to excel, innovate,and make a meaningful impact.

But how do you identify your passions if they're not immediately obvious? Here are a few exercises to get you started:

• **The Time Warp:** Think back to your childhood. What activities did you love? What did you dream of becoming? Often, our early passions hold clues to our inherent interests and talents.

• **The Flow State:** What activities make you lose track of time? When do you feel most "in the zone"? These are often indicators of activities that align with your strengths and passions.

• **The Curiosity Test:** What topics or subjects pique your curiosity? What do you find yourself researching or reading about in your free time? Your natural curiosity can leadyou to unexplored passions.

• **The Values Check:** What values are most important to you? Do you value creativity, collaboration, impact, autonomy? Identifying your core values can help you narrow down career paths that align with your beliefs.

Strengths: Your Superpowers

Your strengths are your unique abilities, the things you do exceptionally well. They're your superpowers, the assets you bringto the table that set you apart from others.

Discovering your strengths isn't just about stroking your ego; it's about understanding what you have to offer the world. When you leverage your strengths, you're not only more likely to succeed, but you're also more likely to find work that's fulfilling and energizing.

Here are a few exercises to help you identify your strengths:

• **The Feedback Loop:** Ask friends, family, colleagues, or mentors for honest feedback on your strengths. What do they see as your greatest assets?

• **The Accomplishment Review:** Look back on your past achievements. What skills or talents did you utilize to achieve those successes?

• **The Skills Assessment:** Take a skills assessment test online or through a career counselor. These tests can providevaluable insights into your strengths and weaknesses.

• **The Strengths Journal:** Keep a journal to track your daily activities. What tasks do you enjoy? What do you find easy or effortless? These are often clues to your underlyingstrengths.

Values: Your Guiding Principles

Values are your deeply held beliefs, the principles that guide your decisions and actions. They're your moral compass, the foundation upon which you build your life and career.

Aligning your career with your values is crucial for long-term happiness and fulfillment. When your work aligns with your values, you'll feel a sense of purpose and meaning, which can leadto greater job satisfaction and overall well-being.

Here are a few exercises to help you clarify your values:

•	**The Values Brainstorm:** Make a list of all the values that are important to you. This could include things like integrity, honesty, creativity, collaboration, or impact.

•	**The Values Prioritization:** Rank your values in order of importance. What are your top three values? These are thevalues that should guide your career decisions.

•	**The Values Reflection:** Think about times in your life whenyou felt most fulfilled or aligned. What values were presentin those situations?

•	**The Values Conflict:** Consider situations where you've felt conflicted or compromised. What values were at odds in those situations?

Putting It All Together

Once you've identified your passions, strengths, and

values, it's time to connect the dots. Look for patterns and themes that emerge. Are there any common threads that link your passions, strengths, and values?

For example, if you're passionate about helping others, have strong communication skills, and value collaboration, a career in healthcare or social work might be a good fit. If you're passionate about technology, have strong analytical skills, and value innovation, a career in software development or engineering might be more aligned.

Remember, this is an ongoing process. Your passions, strengths, and values may evolve over time, so it's important to revisit these exercises periodically to ensure your career path remains aligned with your authentic self.

By taking the time to understand what truly drives you, you'll be well on your way to hiring a boss that not only appreciates your skills but also nurtures your passions and values.

Crystallizing Your Vision

In the previous sections, you embarked on a journey of self-discovery, unearthing your passions, strengths, and values. Now, it's time to synthesize those insights and articulate them into a clear, concise statement that encapsulates your ideal career path. This statement, often referred to as a "career vision statement," will serve as your guiding light, a compass that keeps you focused and motivated throughout your job search and beyond.

Why a Career Vision Statement Matters

Think of your career vision statement as a personal manifesto, a declaration of your professional aspirations. It's a powerful tool that can help you:

• **Clarify Your Goals:** By articulating your ideal career path, you gain a deeper understanding of what you truly want toachieve.

• **Focus Your Search:** A well-defined vision statement helps you target your job search, ensuring that you're pursuing opportunities that align with your goals.

• **Make Informed Decisions:** When faced with career choices, your vision statement provides a benchmark for evaluating which options are the best fit.

• **Communicate with Confidence:** A clear and concise statement allows you to articulate your career aspirations to potential employers, mentors, and network contacts.

Crafting Your Career Vision Statement

There's no one-size-fits-all formula for crafting a career vision statement. It should be as unique as you are, reflecting your individuality and aspirations. However, here are some guidelines to help you get started:

1. **Reflect on Your Passions and Strengths:** What are you truly passionate about? What activities energize you and make you feel fulfilled? What are your natural talents and

skills? Consider the feedback you received from others and the insights you gained from self-reflection exercises.

2. **Identify Your Ideal Work Environment:** What kind of work environment do you thrive in? Do you prefer a fast-paced startup or a more established company? Do you want to work independently or as part of a team? What kind of culture resonates with you?

3. **Envision Your Impact:** What do you want to achieve in your career? How do you want to contribute to the world? What kind of legacy do you want to leave behind? Think big and don't be afraid to dream.

4. **Write a First Draft:** Start by writing a rough draft of your career vision statement. Don't worry about perfection at this stage; just get your thoughts on paper.

5. **Refine and Polish:** Review your draft and make sure it's clear, concise, and specific. Use strong action verbs and avoid jargon. Keep it to one or two sentences.

6. **Get Feedback:** Share your vision statement with trusted friends, mentors, or career coaches. Their feedback can help you refine your statement and ensure that it accurately reflects your goals.

Example Career Vision Statements

To give you some inspiration, here are a few examples of career vision statements:

- "To lead a high-performing team that develops

innovative solutions to improve healthcare access for underservedcommunities."

- "To leverage my expertise in data analysis to drive strategicbusiness decisions and achieve measurable results."

- "To create a sustainable fashion brand that empowers women and promotes ethical practices."

- "To inspire and educate the next generation of engineers through engaging curriculum and hands-on learning experiences."

Your Vision Statement is a Living Document

Remember, your career vision statement isn't set in stone. It's a living document that can and should evolve as you grow and your goals change. Revisit your statement regularly and make adjustments as needed.

Putting Your Vision into Action

Once you have a clear and concise career vision statement, it's time to put it into action. Use it as a guide for your job search, your career development, and your daily decisions.

- **Target Your Search:** Focus your job search on companies and roles that align with your vision statement.

- **Tailor Your Resume:** Highlight the skills and experiences that are most relevant to your desired career path.

- **Ace Your Interviews:** Use your vision statement to

answer questions about your career goals and aspirations.

- **Negotiate with Confidence:** Know your worth and negotiate from a position of strength, always keeping yourvision in mind.

A Vision for Success

Crystallizing your vision is a critical step in the "Hire Your Boss" process. It empowers you to take control of your career, make informed decisions, and pursue opportunities that truly resonate with you.

As the renowned career coach Richard N. Bolles writes in his classic guide *What Color Is Your Parachute?*, "The clearer your vision, the easier your decisions." (Bolles 2023). So, take the time to craft a compelling career vision statement that will serve as your north star on your journey to professional fulfillment. Your future self will thank you.

Additional Tips:

- **Be Authentic:** Your career vision statement should reflect your true passions and aspirations.

- **Be Specific:** Avoid vague language and generalities. The more specific your statement, the more powerful it will be.

- **Be Positive:** Frame your statement in a positive light, focusing on what you want to achieve, not what you want to avoid.

- **Be Bold:** Don't be afraid to aim high and dream

big. Your career vision statement is a reflection of your potential.

Remember, your career vision statement is a powerful tool that can help you achieve your dreams. Use it wisely and watch your career soar.

Chapter 3: Mapping Your Career Vision

Remember that feeling when you were a kid, drawing out elaborate plans for your dream treehouse? The secret tunnels, the rope ladder, the crow's nest overlooking your kingdom? That sense of excitement, possibility, and ownership?

Well, it's time to tap into that childlike wonder and channel it into your career. Because crafting your career vision isn't just about filling out a worksheet; it's about designing a future that genuinely excites you.

In this chapter, we're going to ditch the vague aspirations and create a crystal-clear roadmap for your professional life. We'll move beyond "I want a better job" and dive into the specifics: what kind of work fulfills you, what impact do you want to make, and what environment will help you thrive?

Think of it as building that dream treehouse, but this time, it's your career we're architecting.

Here's what we'll cover:

1.	**Building Your Personal Brand:** We'll discuss how to present a cohesive and authentic professional identity that sets you apart. It's about showcasing your unique value proposition and becoming the obvious choice for your dream job.

2.	**From Vision to Action:** We'll break down your career vision into actionable steps and milestones. No more lofty goals with no plan; it's time to create a concrete roadmap withclear directions.

3.   **Showcasing Your Expertise:** We'll explore how to build an online portfolio or personal website that demonstrates your skills and experience. This is your chance to shine a spotlight on your accomplishments and attract the right opportunities.

By the end of this chapter, you'll have:

•   A vivid and compelling career vision that inspires and motivates you.

•   A clear understanding of your personal brand and how to communicate it effectively.

•   A concrete action plan to guide your career journey.

•   A professional online presence that showcases your skills and expertise.

So, grab your tools and let's start building. It's time to map out your career vision and create a future that fills you with the same excitement as that childhood dream treehouse.

Building Your Personal Brand

"Your brand is what people say about you when you're not in the room." – Jeff Bezos.

In the "Hire Your Boss" framework, personal branding is not just about self-promotion; it's about strategically showcasing your unique value proposition to the world. It's the art of creating a professional identity that's both cohesive and authentically you. Think of it as the narrative that you curate and control, the story you want others to associate with your name.

Why is this crucial?

In today's competitive job market, a strong personal brand sets you apart from the crowd. It helps you attract the right opportunities, build credibility, and ultimately, hire the boss that aligns with your career goals. A well-defined brand creates a lasting impression on potential employers, making you the obvious choice.

Understanding Personal Branding

Personal branding is not about pretending to be someone you're not. It's about identifying your strengths, passions, and unique qualities, and then weaving them into a compelling narrative that resonates with your target audience.

According to William Arruda, a leading expert in personal branding, "Your brand is the emotional experience you want people to have as a result of interacting with you." (Arruda, William. *Digital You: Real Personal Branding in the Virtual Age*. Pearson Education, 2014.) It's about leaving a positive, lasting impact on everyone you encounter, from your LinkedIn connections to your future boss.

Building Blocks of Your Personal Brand

1.   **Your Values:** What are the core principles that guide your life and work? What are the non-negotiables that you stand for? Your values form the foundation of your

personal brand.

2.   **Your Strengths:** What are you naturally good at? What unique skills and experiences do you bring to the table? Your strengths are your superpowers, the assets that make you valuable to potential employers.

3.   **Your Passions:** What are you genuinely excited about? What motivates you to get up in the morning and give it your all? Your passions are your fuel, the driving force behind your career.

Crafting Your Brand Story

Your brand story is the narrative that ties your values, strengths, and passions together. It's the elevator pitch that you can confidently deliver to anyone who asks, "Tell me about yourself."

To craft your brand story, consider these questions:

- What are the key moments or experiences that have shaped your career?

- What are you most proud of achieving?

- What challenges have you overcome?

- What are your aspirations for the future?

Remember, authenticity is key. Don't try to be someone you're not. Instead, focus on presenting the best version of yourself.

Showcasing Your Brand

Once you've crafted your brand story, it's time to share it with theworld. Here are a few channels you can leverage:

1.   **LinkedIn:** Your LinkedIn profile is your online resume, but it's also a platform to showcase your personality and expertise. Use it to share your accomplishments, participate in industry discussions, and connect with other professionals in your field.

2.   **Personal Website or Portfolio:** If you have a creative or technical background, consider building a personal website or portfolio to showcase your work. This is a great way to demonstrate your skills and stand out from other candidates.

3.   **Social Media:** Use social media platforms like Twitter and Instagram to share your insights, engage with your audience, and build a community around your personal brand.

Maintaining Authenticity

It's important to remember that personal branding is an ongoing process. It's not a one-time event, but rather a continuous effort to maintain a consistent and authentic image.

Here are a few tips for staying true to your brand:

- Be genuine in your interactions.

- Share your knowledge and insights generously.

- Be open to feedback and willing to learn.

- Don't be afraid to show your personality.

By staying true to yourself and consistently delivering value, you'll build a strong personal brand that attracts the right opportunities and helps you hire the boss of your dreams.

Remember: Your personal brand is your most valuable asset. Invest in it, nurture it, and let it shine. It's your key to unlocking a fulfilling and successful career.

From Vision to Action

You've crafted a compelling career vision – a vivid picture of where you want to be professionally. It's inspiring, motivating, and... a little daunting. That's perfectly normal. Big dreams often feel far off and overwhelming. But remember, the most ambitious journeys begin with a single step. And the good news is, your career vision isn't just a distant fantasy; it's a roadmap waiting to be explored.

In this section, we'll roll up our sleeves and translate your vision into a concrete action plan. We'll break down those big dreams into manageable steps, set clear milestones, and equip you with the tools to turn your aspirations into tangible achievements.

The Power of Goal Setting

Goals are the fuel that propels us forward. They provide direction, focus, and a sense of purpose. Without them, we're like ships without rudders, drifting aimlessly in the vast ocean of possibilities. But not all goals are created equal. Effective goals areSMART:

• **Specific:** Clearly defined and focused. Instead of "I want to be successful," try "I want to be promoted to senior marketing manager within two years."

• **Measurable:** Quantifiable and trackable. "I want to increase sales" becomes "I want to increase sales by 15%in the next quarter."

• **Achievable:** Realistic and attainable. While ambition is admirable, setting unrealistic goals can lead to frustration and discouragement.

• **Relevant:** Aligned with your overall career vision. Each goal should be a stepping stone towards your ultimate destination.

• **Time-Bound:** With a specific deadline. This creates a senseof urgency and helps you stay on track.

By setting SMART goals, you transform your vision from a vague aspiration into a series of concrete targets. This not only makes your dreams feel more attainable but also provides a clear roadmap for your journey.

Breaking Down Your Vision

Now that you understand the importance of SMART goals, let's break down your career vision into actionable steps. Think of this as reverse engineering your dream job. Start by identifying the key milestones you need to reach to achieve your vision. These could include:

• **Acquiring new skills or certifications:** What specific skills or knowledge do you need to gain to qualify for your desired role?

• **Gaining relevant experience:** What type of experience would make you a stronger candidate? Can you get it through volunteering, internships, or side projects?

• **Building your network:** Who can help you on your journey? How can you connect with influential people in your field?

• **Landing a specific job or promotion:** What specific position or level of responsibility do you need to reach to achieve your vision?

Once you've identified your milestones, break them down further into smaller, more manageable steps. These could include:

• **Enrolling in a course or program:** Research and sign up for a training program to develop the necessary skills.

• **Applying for specific jobs or internships:** Tailor your resume and cover letter to highlight your relevant experience and skills.

• **Attending industry events or conferences:** Network with professionals in your field and learn about new trends and opportunities.

• **Seeking mentorship or coaching:** Find someone

who can provide guidance and support on your career journey.

By breaking down your vision into smaller steps, you'll create a clear path forward and avoid feeling overwhelmed. Each step, no matter how small, is a victory that brings you closer to your goal.

Creating a Timeline

Now that you have a list of actionable steps, it's time to create a timeline. This will help you stay organized, prioritize tasks, and track your progress. Assign a realistic deadline to each step, taking into account your other commitments and responsibilities. Remember, this is a working document, so feel free to adjust it as needed.

Staying Motivated

The journey to achieving your career vision can be long and challenging. It's easy to lose momentum or get discouraged along the way. That's why it's crucial to stay motivated and keep your eyes on the prize. Here are a few tips:

- **Visualize your success:** Imagine yourself achieving your goals and enjoying the rewards of your hard work.

- **Set reminders:** Write down your goals and post them where you'll see them every day. Use a calendar or app to set reminders for upcoming deadlines.

- **Celebrate milestones:** Acknowledge and reward yourself for each step you take towards your vision. This will reinforce positive behavior and keep you motivated.

- **Find a support system:** Surround yourself with people who believe in you and your dreams. Share your goals with them and ask for their support.

- **Don't give up:** There will be setbacks and obstacles along the way. Remember, failure is not the opposite of success; it's part of the process. Learn from your mistakes, adjust your course, and keep moving forward.

By following these steps and staying committed to your vision, you'll be well on your way to hiring your boss and creating the career of your dreams. Remember, the power to shape your future is in your hands.

Showcasing Your Expertise

Think of your online presence as a digital storefront. It's your 24/7 opportunity to display your finest wares—your skills, experience, and the unique value you offer. In today's job market, having an online portfolio or personal website isn't just a nice-to-have, it's a necessity. It's your chance to make a memorable first impression and stand out from the competition.

Why You Need a Digital Portfolio

A well-crafted online portfolio serves multiple purposes:

- **Evidence of Your Skills:** It's not enough to say

you're a great writer, designer, or developer. A portfolio shows potential employers what you can actually do.

• **Proof of Your Expertise:** It allows you to go beyond your resume, providing a deeper dive into your projects and accomplishments.

• **A Platform for Your Personal Brand:** It's a space to showcase your personality, your passion, and your unique style.

• **A Magnet for Opportunities:** A strong online presence can attract recruiters and potential clients who might not have found you otherwise.

The Power of Show, Don't Tell

Remember the adage, "Actions speak louder than words"? This is especially true when it comes to showcasing your expertise. A portfolio allows you to move beyond listing skills on a resume and actually demonstrate your capabilities in action.

For example, if you're a writer, you can share samples of your best articles or blog posts. If you're a designer, you can showcase your most creative projects. And if you're a developer, you can highlight your most innovative code contributions.

Choosing Your Platform

There are many different platforms you can use to create your online portfolio. Some popular options include:

- **Portfolio Websites:** These platforms are specifically designed for showcasing creative work and often offer customizable templates. Examples include Wix, Squarespace, and Cargo.

- **Personal Websites:** You can create your own website using WordPress, which offers more flexibility but also requires more technical knowledge.

- **LinkedIn:** While primarily a networking platform, LinkedIn allows you to upload your resume, projects, and publications, making it a good option for professionals in any field.

The best platform for you will depend on your budget, your technical skills, and the type of work you want to showcase.

Building Your Portfolio: Essential Elements

Regardless of the platform you choose, there are certain elementsthat every strong portfolio should include:

- **About Me Section:** This is your chance to introduce yourself, share your story, and highlight your passions and goals.

- **Work Samples:** Choose your best work and present it in a visually appealing way. Include project descriptions, your role in each project, and any relevant results or outcomes.

- **Contact Information:** Make it easy for potential

employersor clients to get in touch with you.

- **Call to Action:** Encourage visitors to take the next step, whether that's contacting you for a job interview or hiring you for a project.

Curating Your Content: Less is More

It's tempting to include everything you've ever done in your portfolio, but remember that quality is more important than quantity. Choose your most impressive and relevant work samples and present them in a way that highlights your strengths and accomplishments.

Tips for Creating a Standout Portfolio

- **Keep It Updated:** Your portfolio should be a living document that evolves as you gain new skills and experiences.

- **Tell a Story:** Use your portfolio to tell the story of your career and your passions.

- **Make It Easy to Navigate:** Ensure your portfolio is user-friendly and easy to navigate.

- **Get Feedback:** Ask friends, colleagues, or mentors to review your portfolio and provide constructive feedback.

Don't Let Perfection Be the Enemy of Good

Remember, your portfolio doesn't have to be perfect to be effective. The most important thing is to start somewhere and continue to iterate and improve over time.

Building a strong online portfolio takes time and effort, but it's an investment that will pay off in the long run. By showcasing your expertise and creating a platform for your personal brand, you'll be well on your way to hiring your boss and landing your dream job.

Additional Resources

• How to Make a Portfolio in 10 Steps: https://www.wix.com/blog/how-to-make-online-design-portfolio-guide

• How to Build an Online Portfolio In 30 Minutes or Less: https://www.format.com/magazine/resources/design/how-to-build-online-portfolio-easy-guide

By following these tips and utilizing the resources available, you can create a compelling online portfolio that showcases your expertise and sets you apart in the job market.

Part II: The "Hire Your Boss" Blueprint

Chapter 4: Positioning 101: Becoming the Obvious Choice

Picture this: You're a hiring manager sifting through a stack of nearly identical resumes. Each one boasts the same buzzwords, the same skills, the same vague promises of "excellence." Sound familiar?

In today's competitive job market, simply having the right qualifications isn't enough. You need to stand out, to differentiateyourself, to become the undeniable choice. That's where Positioning comes in.

Think of Positioning as your professional spotlight. It's about strategically crafting your narrative, highlighting your unique strengths, and showcasing the specific value you bring to the table. It's about becoming the candidate who not only meets the requirements, but exceeds expectations.

In this chapter, we're going to dive deep into the art of Positioning. We'll explore:

- **Why Positioning Matters:** Uncover how strategic positioning can make you the top candidate, even if you don't have the "perfect" resume.

- **Crafting Your Elevator Pitch:** Learn how to succinctly communicate your value proposition in a way that leaves alasting impression.

- **Building Your Personal Brand:** Discover how to cultivate a professional identity that aligns with your career goals andresonates with employers.

- **Networking Strategically:** Harness the power of your network to amplify your message and open doors to hidden opportunities.

By the end of this chapter, you'll have a clear understanding of how to position yourself as the obvious choice for your dream job. You'll be able to confidently articulate your value, showcase your expertise, and leave a lasting impression on anyone you meet.

So, are you ready to take your job search to the next level? Let's dive in and discover the power of Positioning.

Standing Out in the Crowd

In the bustling marketplace of job seekers, you're not just another face in the crowd. You're a unique individual with a distinct set of skills, experiences, and aspirations. But how do you communicate this uniqueness to potential employers? How do you ensure that you don't get lost in a sea of resumes and applications? The answer lies in mastering the art of positioning.

What is Positioning?

Positioning, in the context of your career, is the process of deliberately crafting and presenting your professional identity to occupy a distinct and valuable space in the minds of potential employers. It's about showcasing your unique value proposition and differentiating yourself from the competition.

Think of it as your personal branding strategy. Just as companies create brands to stand out in the market, you need to create a personal brand that communicates your strengths, expertise, and what makes you the ideal candidate for your dream job.

Why Positioning Matters

In today's competitive job market, a strong personal brand is moreimportant than ever. It helps you:

1.   **Attract the right opportunities:** When you clearly articulate your value proposition, you attract employers who are looking for exactly what you offer.

2.   **Stand out from the competition:** A well-defined personal brand makes you memorable and helps you differentiate yourself from other candidates.

3.   **Command higher compensation:** When you position yourself as an expert in your field, you're in a better position to negotiate for higher salaries and better benefits.

4.   **Build a strong professional network:** A strong personal brand attracts like-minded individuals and helps you build valuable relationships.

How to Define Your Positioning

Defining your positioning requires a deep understanding of your strengths, skills, experiences, and career goals. Here's a step-by-step guide to help you get started:

1.   **Self-Assessment:** Start by conducting a thorough self-assessment. Identify your core strengths, areas of expertise, and what you enjoy doing most. Consider taking personality tests or seeking feedback from trusted colleagues or mentors.

2.   **Identify Your Target Audience:** Who are the employers you want to attract? What are their needs and pain points? Understanding your target audience will help you tailor your message and positioning accordingly.

3.   **Craft Your Unique Value Proposition:** Based on your self-assessment and target audience, articulate your unique value proposition. What specific skills and experiences do you bring to the table? How can you help employers solve their problems or achieve their goals?

4.   **Develop Your Personal Brand Message:** Create a concise and compelling message that encapsulates your unique value proposition. This message should be consistent across all your professional materials and communication channels.

5.   **Showcase Your Expertise:** Demonstrate your expertise through your resume, LinkedIn profile, portfolio, personal website, and any other relevant channels. Share your knowledge through blog posts, articles, or social media posts.

Positioning in Action

Let's take a look at a few examples of how effective positioningcan make a difference in your job search:

•	**Example 1:** A software engineer with a passion for user experience (UX) positions herself as a "UX-focused software engineer." This differentiates her from other engineers who may be more focused on technical aspects, making her more attractive to companies that prioritize user experience.

•	**Example 2:** A marketing professional with a strong track record in social media marketing positions himself as a "social media strategist." This highlights his expertise in a specific area, making him a valuable asset to companies seeking to enhance their social media presence.

•	**Example 3:** A financial analyst with a deep understanding of sustainable investing positions herself as a "sustainable finance expert." This positions her as a leader in a growing field and attracts employers who are committed to responsible investing.

The Power of Differentiation

In a crowded job market, differentiation is key to success. When you clearly define your positioning, you're not just another job seeker; you're a solution provider, a problem solver, a valuable asset. You're someone who stands out from the crowd and makesa lasting impression.

As William Arruda, a personal branding expert, puts it,

"In today's world, your personal brand is your reputation. It's what people say about you when you're not in the room." (Arruda, *Ditch. Dare. Do!* 2015)

By taking control of your personal brand and positioning yourself strategically, you can shape the narrative of your career and attract the opportunities you deserve.

Remember, you're not just looking for a job; you're hiring your boss. And to hire the right boss, you need to position yourself as the right candidate.

Now, it's your turn to shine. Define your positioning, differentiate yourself, and take the next step towards your dream job. The power is in your hands.

Crafting Your Elevator Pitch

Picture this: You're in an elevator with the CEO of your dream company. The doors are about to close, and you have 30 seconds to make an impression. What do you say?

This is the essence of the elevator pitch – a brief, compelling summary of who you are, what you do, and what you can offer. It's your chance to spark interest, showcase your value, and leave a lasting impression.

But crafting a powerful elevator pitch isn't about reciting a rehearsed script. It's about distilling your unique value proposition into a concise and impactful message. It's your 30-second career commercial, designed to capture attention and leave your audience wanting more.

The Anatomy of a Powerful Elevator Pitch

A successful elevator pitch typically includes the following elements:

1. **Hook:** Start with a captivating opening line that grabs attention and piques curiosity.

2. **Introduction:** Briefly introduce yourself and your professional background.

3. **Unique Value Proposition:** Highlight your key skills, experiences, and accomplishments that set you apart.

4. **Call to Action:** End with a clear call to action, inviting further conversation or connection.

Examples of Elevator Pitches

Let's look at a few examples to illustrate how to apply theseelements:

- **Marketing Professional:** "I'm a data-driven marketing strategist with a proven track record of launching successful campaigns that drive revenue growth. I'm passionate about leveraging data and insights to craft innovative solutions that resonate with target audiences."

- **Software Engineer:** "I'm a full-stack software engineer with expertise in building scalable and user-friendly applications. I'm excited about using technology to solve real-world problems and create meaningful experiencesfor users."

- **Healthcare Professional:** "I'm a compassionate

nurse with a passion for patient advocacy and a strong understanding of healthcare operations. I'm committed to delivering high-quality care and improving patient outcomes."

Tailoring Your Pitch to Your Audience

One size doesn't fit all when it comes to elevator pitches. You'll need to tailor your pitch to your specific audience and context. Forexample:

• **Networking Events:** Focus on building rapport and making a connection.

• **Job Interviews:** Highlight your skills and experiences that align with the job requirements.

• **Career Fairs:** Be prepared to quickly summarize your qualifications and career goals.

Tips for Crafting a Compelling Elevator Pitch

• **Keep It Concise:** Aim for 30-60 seconds.

• **Use Strong Verbs:** Action words like "created," "led," "managed," and "achieved" make your pitch more impactful.

• **Quantify Your Accomplishments:** Use numbers and metrics to demonstrate your impact. For example, instead of saying "increased sales," say "increased sales by 20%."

• **Focus on Results:** Highlight the positive outcomes of your work, not just your responsibilities.

- **Practice, Practice, Practice:** Rehearse your pitch until itfeels natural and conversational.

- **Be Confident:** Speak with enthusiasm and conviction. Yourpassion will shine through.

Avoiding Common Pitfalls

- **Don't ramble:** Stick to the essentials.

- **Don't be vague:** Use specific examples to illustrate your skills and experience.

- **Don't be overly modest:** This is your chance to shine, so don't be afraid to highlight your achievements.

- **Don't forget your call to action:** Invite further conversationor connection.

The Power of Storytelling

One effective way to make your elevator pitch memorable is to incorporate a brief anecdote or story. This can help you connect with your audience on a personal level and demonstrate your unique personality and values. For example:

"I'm a graphic designer with a passion for creating visually stunning designs that tell a story. I recently worked on a project for a non-profit organization, where I designed a series of infographics that helped them raise awareness about their cause and increase donations by 30%."

Practice Makes Perfect

The more you practice your elevator pitch, the more comfortable and confident you'll become. Practice in front of a mirror, record yourself, or ask a friend or colleague for feedback. The goal is to deliver your pitch in a way that's natural, engaging, and authentic.

Your Elevator Pitch: Your Secret Weapon

A well-crafted elevator pitch is a powerful tool in your job search arsenal. It can open doors to new opportunities, spark meaningful conversations, and help you land your dream job. So, take the time to craft a pitch that truly reflects your unique value, and be prepared to use it whenever the opportunity arises. Remember, you never know who you might meet in the elevator.

Networking Strategically

Your network is one of the most powerful tools in your job search arsenal. But it's not just about collecting business cards or amassing LinkedIn connections. It's about strategically building relationships that can open doors, provide insights, and elevate your professional standing.

Networking isn't about schmoozing or being fake. It's about genuine connection, mutual support, and building a community of like-minded professionals who can help you achieve your goals. When done right, networking can be a game-changer in your "Hire Your Boss" journey.

Why Networking Matters

In today's competitive job market, who you know often matters asmuch as what you know. Research shows that up to 85% of jobs are filled through networking (Bolles, 2017). This means that tapping into your network can give you a significant advantage over other candidates who are relying solely on online job boards and traditional applications.

Your network can:

• **Provide insider information:** Your contacts can alert you tounadvertised job openings, give you insights into company culture, and even offer tips on how to impress specific hiring managers.

• **Offer referrals and recommendations:** A personal recommendation from someone within a company can significantly increase your chances of getting an interview.

• **Boost your credibility:** Being connected to influential people in your field can enhance your professional reputation and make you a more attractive candidate.

• **Open doors to new opportunities:** Networking can lead to unexpected opportunities, such as freelance projects, speaking engagements, or mentorship programs.

How to Leverage Your Network

Here's a step-by-step guide on how to use your network strategically:

1. **Identify Your Target Network:** Think about the people who could be most helpful in your job search. This

could include former colleagues, mentors, classmates, professors, industry experts, recruiters, and even friends and family.

2.	**Reach Out with a Clear Purpose:** Don't just send a generic message saying, "I'm looking for a job." Be specific about the type of role you're seeking, the companies you're interested in, and the kind of help you're looking for (e.g., information, advice, referrals).

3.	**Offer Value:** Networking is a two-way street. Don't just ask for help; offer something in return. This could be sharing an article, making an introduction, or simply offering a listening ear.

4.	**Be Authentic and Personable:** People are more likely to help someone they like and trust. Be yourself, show genuine interest in others, and build relationships based on mutual respect.

5.	**Follow Up and Stay Connected:** Don't just disappear after you get what you need. Stay in touch with your contacts, send updates on your job search, and continue to offer value.

Networking Tips and Strategies

•	**Attend Industry Events:** Conferences, workshops, and meetups are great places to meet new people and expand your network.

•	**Join Online Communities:** LinkedIn groups,

Facebook groups, and online forums can be valuable sources of information and connections.

- **Leverage Your Alumni Network:** Your school's alumni association can be a goldmine of potential contacts.

- **Use Informational Interviews:** These are informal conversations with people working in your field of interest. They can provide valuable insights and help you build relationships.

- **Be a Connector:** Introduce people in your network who could benefit from knowing each other. This can help you build a reputation as someone who is helpful and resourceful.

Networking Etiquette

- **Be Respectful of People's Time:** Don't overstay yourwelcome or bombard people with messages.

- **Be Prepared:** Have your elevator pitch ready and be ableto articulate your goals and skills clearly.

- **Be Gracious:** Always say thank you for any help or adviceyou receive.

- **Be Professional:** Maintain a professional demeanor, evenin informal settings.

References

Bolles, Richard N. 2017. *What Color Is Your Parachute? 2018: A Practical Manual for Job-Hunters and Career-Changers.*

Berkeley, CA: Ten Speed Press.

Your Network is Your Net Worth

By investing time and effort in building a strong professional network, you're not just enhancing your job search prospects; you're investing in your long-term career success. Remember, your network is your net worth. Nurture it, leverage it, and watch it open doors you never thought possible.

Chapter 5: Crafting Your Unique Value Proposition

Forget about being just another name on a stack of resumes. It's time to unleash your secret weapon – your Unique Value Proposition (UVP). This isn't just about listing your skills; it's about proving you're the solution to an employer's problems.

Think of it like this: your dream job is out there looking for someone to solve a specific challenge. Your UVP is the beacon thatsignals, "I'm the one you need!" It's the difference between blending in with the crowd and becoming the obvious choice.

In this chapter, we'll dive deep into what a UVP is, why it's crucial for "hiring your boss," and how to craft one that makes you irresistible to employers. We'll move beyond generic buzzwords and help you articulate the tangible results you bring to the table.

You'll learn how to:

• **Uncover your superpowers:** Identify the unique combination of skills, experiences, and qualities that make you stand out.

• **Translate skills into solutions:** Clearly articulate how your abilities directly address the challenges your target companies face.

• **Tailor your message:** Customize your resume and

cover letter to showcase your UVP for each specific job.

• **Speak the language of results:** Quantify your accomplishments and highlight the impact you've made in previous roles.

By the end of this chapter, you'll have a powerful UVP that not only gets you noticed but also positions you as the candidate who can deliver real results. Get ready to transform your job search from a game of chance into a strategic pursuit of the perfect match.

Let's unlock your full potential and show the world what you're truly capable of.

Solving Problems, Not Filling Roles

Imagine two candidates vying for the same marketing manager position.

Candidate A's resume is a laundry list of skills: proficient in SEO, content marketing, social media, email marketing, and data analytics. Impressive, right?

Now, consider Candidate B. Their resume tells a different story. It doesn't just list skills; it showcases achievements. It highlights how they increased website traffic by 30% through targeted SEO campaigns, boosted social media engagement by 50% with a creative content strategy, and generated $100,000 in revenue through a successful email marketing campaign.

Who do you think stands out?

If you're like most hiring managers, you're drawn to Candidate B. Why? Because they don't just tell you what they can do; they show you the value they bring to the table.

The Problem with the Skills-Focused Resume

The traditional resume, with its emphasis on skills and experience, has become outdated. It's a one-size-fits-all approach that fails to capture your unique value proposition. It's like trying to sell a house by listing its square footage and number of bedrooms, without mentioning the stunning views, the gourmet kitchen, or the charming backyard oasis.

Sure, skills are important. But they're just the starting point. What truly matters to employers is how you use those skills to solve problems, achieve results, and contribute to their bottom line.

The "Hire Your Boss" Approach

In the "Hire Your Boss" framework, we shift the focus from skills to value-add. Instead of simply listing your qualifications, you highlight your accomplishments, your impact, and your ability to deliver results.

This approach requires a mindset shift. It's about seeing yourself not as a job seeker, but as a problem solver. It's about understanding the challenges your potential employer faces and positioning yourself as the solution.

How to Showcase Your Value-Add

1.   **Quantify Your Accomplishments:** Don't just say you're a "results-oriented" marketer. Show how you increased sales by 20%, reduced customer acquisition costs by 15%, or launched a new product that generated $50,000 in revenue within the first month. Use numbers to make your achievements tangible and impactful.

2.   **Tell a Story:** Don't just list your responsibilities in previous roles. Craft a narrative that demonstrates your problem-solving skills and your ability to overcome challenges. Use the STAR method (Situation, Task, Action, Result) to structure your stories and highlight your impact.

3.   **Tailor Your Message:** Don't send out generic resumes and cover letters. Customize your application materials for each specific job you apply for. Research the company, understand their needs, and explain how your skills and experience can help them achieve their goals.

4.   **Focus on the "So What?":** Don't just list your skills and accomplishments. Explain the "so what?" – the impact of your work on the company's bottom line. Did you save the company money? Increase efficiency? Improve customer satisfaction? Make sure your potential employer understands the value you bring.

5.   **Leverage Testimonials and References:** Don't just rely on your own words to showcase your value. Gather testimonials from colleagues, supervisors, or clients who can attest to your skills and accomplishments. Provide references

who can speak to your work ethic, your problem-solving abilities, and your overall contribution to the team.

Examples of Value-Add Statements

• Instead of: "Proficient in social media marketing," say: "Increased social media engagement by 50% through a targeted content strategy, resulting in a 20% increase in website traffic and a 10% increase in leads."

• Instead of: "Experienced project manager," say: "Successfully led a cross-functional team to launch a new product on time and under budget, generating $100,000 in revenue within the first quarter."

• Instead of: "Strong communication skills," say: "Developed and implemented a comprehensive communication plan that improved employee engagement by 30% and reduced turnover by 10%."

The Power of Value-Add

By focusing on your value-add, you're not just applying for jobs; you're creating opportunities. You're positioning yourself as a valuable asset, a problem solver, and a potential leader. You're demonstrating your worth and making yourself irresistible to potential employers.

Remember:

• The "Hire Your Boss" framework is about empowerment, not entitlement.

• You're not demanding a job; you're showcasing your

value and finding the right fit.

- By focusing on what you bring to the table, you're not just getting hired; you're choosing a company and a boss that will help you thrive.

So, the next time you update your resume or prepare for aninterview, ask yourself: "Am I just listing my skills, or am I demonstrating my value-add?"

Shift your focus, and watch your job search transform.

Tailoring Your Message

In the competitive job market, a generic resume and cover letter won't cut it. To capture the attention of potential employers and showcase your alignment with their needs, you need to tailor your message to each specific opportunity. Think of it as a bespoke suit— it's made to fit you perfectly and complements your unique style.

The Power of Customization

Imagine receiving two gifts: one is a generic, store-bought item with a pre-written card, while the other is a thoughtful, personalized gift with a handwritten note expressing the giver's understanding of your interests and preferences. Which one would make you feel more valued and appreciated? The same principle applies to job applications.

A customized resume and cover letter demonstrate your genuine interest in the position and the company. It shows that you've taken the time to research the role, understand its requirements, and tailor your message accordingly. This level of effort sets you apart from other applicants who may have simply submitted a generic application.

Resumes: Showcasing Your Value

Your resume is your marketing brochure, highlighting your skills, experiences, and accomplishments. It's your first chance to make a strong impression and convince employers that you're the right fit for the job. To maximize its impact, follow these customization tips:

1.   **Mirror the Job Description:** Carefully read the job description and identify the key skills and qualifications the employer is seeking. Then, tailor your resume to emphasize those specific areas. For instance, if the job posting mentions "project management" as a requirement, highlight your project management experience and successes.

2.   **Use Keywords:** Many companies use Applicant Tracking Systems (ATS) to filter resumes based on specific keywords. Incorporate relevant keywords from the job description into your resume to increase your chances of getting noticed by the ATS. However, avoid keyword stuffing, as it can make your resume appear unnatural and spammy.(Smith 2023, 115)

3.   **Quantify Your Accomplishments:** Instead of simply listing your responsibilities, quantify your achievements whenever possible. Use numbers, percentages,

or other metrics to demonstrate the impact you've made in previous roles. For example, instead of saying "managed social media accounts," you could say "increased social media engagement by 25% within six months."

4.   **Tailor Your Skills Section:** Don't just list generic skills. Instead, focus on the specific skills required for the job and provide evidence of your proficiency in those areas. For instance, if the job requires data analysis skills, mention the specific software you've used and the results you've achieved.

5.   **Keep it Concise and Relevant:** Your resume should be no more than two pages long. Focus on your most recent and relevant experience, and omit anything that's not directly applicable to the job.

Cover Letters: Telling Your Story

Your cover letter is your opportunity to tell your story, connect with the employer on a personal level, and explain why you're the perfect candidate for the job. To make it compelling, follow these customization tips:

1.   **Address a Specific Person:** Whenever possible, address your cover letter to a specific person (e.g., the hiring manager or the recruiter). This shows that you've done your research and are genuinely interested in the company.

2.   **Show Your Enthusiasm:** Express your enthusiasm for the position and the company. Explain why you're excited about the opportunity and how your skills and experience

align with the company's goals and values.

3.   **Highlight Your Fit:** Use specific examples from your experience to demonstrate how you meet the job requirements. Don't just reiterate your resume; instead, provide context and detail to showcase your accomplishments and the value you can bring to the company.

4.   **Connect the Dots:** Explain how your past experiences have prepared you for this specific role. For instance, if you're applying for a marketing position, you could discuss how your previous experience in sales helped you develop strong communication and persuasion skills.

5.   **End with a Call to Action:** In your closing paragraph, express your interest in an interview and reiterate your enthusiasm for the position. You can also mention your availability for an interview or a follow-up conversation.

Case Study: The Power of Personalization

To illustrate the effectiveness of customization, let's consider the story of Sarah, a recent graduate with a degree in marketing. Sarah applied for numerous marketing positions, but she wasn't getting any responses. Frustrated, she decided to revamp her approach. Instead of sending generic applications, she meticulously tailored each resume and cover letter to the specific job posting.

In her cover letters, Sarah addressed the hiring manager

by name, expressed her passion for the company's products, and highlighted specific examples of how her skills and experience aligned with the job requirements. She even mentioned a recent marketing campaign the company had launched and offered insights on how she could contribute to future initiatives.

The results were astounding. Sarah started receiving interview invitations, and within a few weeks, she landed her dream job at a leading marketing agency. The key to her success? Personalization.

Going the Extra Mile

In addition to tailoring your resume and cover letter, consider going the extra mile to demonstrate your interest in the company. This could involve:

• **Following the company on social media:** Stay updated on the company's latest news and developments.

• **Engaging with company representatives:** Connect with employees on LinkedIn or attend company events to learn more about the culture and the work environment.

• **Sending a personalized follow-up email:** After submitting your application, send a brief email to the hiring manager or recruiter to reiterate your interest and express your eagerness to discuss your qualifications further.

By putting in the extra effort to tailor your message and

demonstrate your genuine interest, you'll increase your chances of landing an interview and ultimately, hiring your boss.

Remember:

Customization is key to standing out in the competitive job market. Tailor your resume and cover letter to each specific opportunity, and go the extra mile to demonstrate your genuine interest in the company. This will not only increase your chances of getting hired but also ensure that you find a job that truly aligns with your career goals and aspirations.

Keywords and Achievements

Your resume is not just a list of your work history; it's your marketing brochure, your chance to grab the attention of potential bosses and show them exactly why you're the perfect fit. But in today's competitive job market, simply listing your job duties won't cut it. You need to make your resume sing with relevant keywords and quantifiable achievements that demonstrate your impact.

Think of it like this: Your resume is a search engine optimization (SEO) project. Just as websites optimize their content to rank higher in search results, you need to optimize your resume to catch the eye of Applicant Tracking Systems (ATS) and hiring managers.

The Power of Keywords

Keywords are the specific words and phrases that recruiters and hiring managers use to search for candidates. They're like the secret code that unlocks the door to your dream job. But how do you find the right keywords? It's easier than you might think.

1.   **Analyze Job Descriptions:** Start by carefully reading the job descriptions of positions that interest you. Highlight the recurring words and phrases that describe the skills, experience, and qualifications they're looking for. These are your keywords.

2.   **Industry Buzzwords:** Research industry-specific terms and jargon that are relevant to your field. Incorporate these buzzwords into your resume to show that you're in the know.

3.   **Tools and Technologies:** If you have experience with specific software, programming languages, or tools, be sure to mention them by name. This can make you stand out to hiring managers who are looking for candidates with specific technical skills.

For example, if you're applying for a marketing position, your resume might include keywords like "digital marketing," "content creation," "social media strategy," "SEO," or "PPC."

Quantifiable Achievements: Show, Don't Tell

Keywords are essential, but they're only half the battle. To truly make your resume stand out, you need to back up those keywords with concrete evidence of your achievements. This is where quantifiable achievements come in.

Quantifiable achievements are specific, measurable results that you've accomplished in your previous roles. They go beyond simply listing your job duties and tell a story of your impact.

Instead of saying, "Managed social media accounts," try saying, "Increased social media engagement by 25% in six months through targeted campaigns and content creation."

See the difference? The second statement is much more powerful because it quantifies your accomplishment and demonstrates your impact.

Here are some tips for crafting impactful quantifiable achievements:

• **Use Numbers:** Whenever possible, use numbers to quantify your results. This could include percentages, dollar amounts, time saved, or any other measurable metric.

• **Focus on Results:** Highlight the positive outcomes of your actions, not just the tasks you performed.

• **Be Specific:** Avoid vague statements like "improved efficiency" or "increased sales." Be specific about what you achieved and how you did it.

Weaving Keywords and Achievements Together

Now that you understand the importance of keywords

and quantifiable achievements, it's time to weave them together seamlessly into your resume. Here's how:

• **Keywords in Context:** Use keywords strategically throughout your resume, incorporating them into your work experience descriptions, skills section, and even your summary statement.

• **Achievements as Proof:** After each keyword, follow up with a quantifiable achievement that demonstrates your expertise in that area.

• **Tailor to the Job:** Customize your resume for each job application, highlighting the keywords and achievements that are most relevant to the specific role.

Example: Before and After

Let's take a look at a real-world example. Here's a before and after of a marketing manager's resume:

Before:

- Managed social media accounts
- Developed marketing campaigns
- Created content for website and blog

After:

- Increased social media engagement by 25% in six months through targeted campaigns and content creation.
- Developed and executed multi-channel marketing

campaigns that generated $50,000 in revenue.

- Created engaging content for website and blog, resulting in a 15% increase in website traffic.

Notice how the "after" version is much more impactful? It uses keywords in context and backs them up with quantifiable achievements that demonstrate the candidate's skills and experience.

Additional Tips:

- **Use Action Verbs:** Start your achievement statements with strong action verbs like "increased," "developed," "executed," or "created."

- **Keep It Concise:** Each achievement statement should be brief and to the point, focusing on the most relevant details.

- **Proofread Carefully:** Double-check your resume for anytypos or grammatical errors. A polished resume makes a great first impression.

By incorporating relevant keywords and quantifiable achievements, your resume will not only pass the ATS test but alsocaptivate hiring managers and land you an interview.

Remember, your resume is your chance to shine. Make it count!

Chapter 6: Alignment: The Key to Cultural Fit

Imagine this: You've landed your dream job. The salary is great, the benefits are top-notch, and your resume looks amazing with this new title. But a few months in, something feels... off. You dread going to work. You feel like a square peg trying to fit into a round hole. The company culture just isn't a good match for your personality or values.

Sound familiar? You're not alone. Many job seekers focus so much on landing the offer that they overlook a critical factor: alignment.

What is Alignment, Anyway?

Alignment is about finding a workplace that feels like home. It's about finding a company whose values, mission, and work environment resonate with your own. It's about working with people who inspire you and challenge you to be your best. It's about feeling like you belong.

And it's not just about making you happy (although that's a big part of it). Alignment also affects your performance. When you're in a job that aligns with your values and interests, you're more engaged, motivated, and productive. You're more likely to go above and beyond, to innovate, and to make a real impact.

Why Alignment Matters More Than Ever

In today's rapidly changing job market, cultural fit is more important than ever. Companies are realizing that a diverse and inclusive workforce leads to better ideas, greater innovation, and ultimately, more success. They're looking for employees who not only have the right skills but also fit in with their company culture.

And you, as a job seeker, should be looking for the same thing. After all, you're spending a significant portion of your life at work. Shouldn't it be somewhere you feel valued, respected, and energized?

Finding Your Perfect Match

In this chapter, we'll dive deep into the concept of alignment. You'll learn how to:

- **Identify your core values:** What's important to you in a workplace? Collaboration? Autonomy? Social impact? Figure out what makes you tick.

- **Research company culture:** Don't just rely on job descriptions. Dig deeper into a company's mission, values, and employee reviews to get a sense of their culture.

- **Ask the right questions:** During interviews, ask probing questions about the company culture and how employees feel about working there.

- **Trust your gut:** If something feels off, it probably is. Don't ignore red flags just because a job seems perfect on paper.

By prioritizing alignment in your job search, you'll set yourself up for long-term success and happiness. You'll find a workplace that fuels your passion, supports your growth, and feels like home.

Ready to find your perfect match? Let's dive in!

Beyond the Job Description

Let's be honest, the job description is just the tip of the iceberg. It tells you the skills required, the responsibilities involved, maybe a fancy title—but it barely scratches the surface of what it's actually like to work at that company. To truly "hire your boss" and find a job you'll thrive in, you need to go beyond the bullet points and assess the company's culture and values.

Why Cultural Fit Matters

Think of company culture as the personality of an organization. It's the unwritten code of conduct, the unspoken norms, the collective energy that permeates the workplace. It's the difference between feeling energized and engaged at work versus feeling drained and disengaged.

According to a study by Glassdoor, 77% of adults would consider a company's culture before applying for a job there. And for good reason. When your values align with your company's, you're more likely to:

- **Feel a sense of belonging and purpose:** You're not just working for a paycheck; you're contributing to something you believe in.

- **Be more productive and engaged:** You're motivated to do your best work because you're passionate about the company's mission.

- **Enjoy coming to work every day:** You're surrounded by people who share your values and outlook on life.

- **Stay with the company longer:** You're less likely to jump ship when the going gets tough because you're invested in the company's success.

In short, cultural fit is the secret sauce that transforms a job into a fulfilling career.

How to Assess Company Culture

Now, you might be wondering, "How do I actually figure out a company's culture?" It's not always easy, but there are several strategies you can use:

1.   **Do Your Research:** Start by reading the company's website, blog, and social media pages. Look for clues about their values, mission, and overall vibe. Check out review sites like Glassdoor and Indeed to see what current and former employees have to say.

2.   **Talk to People:** If you know anyone who works at the company, pick their brain about the culture. Ask them what they like and dislike about working there, what the management style is like, and how the company supports its

employees.

3.   **Attend Events:** If possible, attend company events or conferences to get a feel for the atmosphere and the people.

4.   **Ask Questions During the Interview:** Don't be afraid to askquestions about the company culture during your interview. This shows that you're genuinely interested in finding the right fit.

Questions to Ask About Company Culture

Here are a few questions you can ask to get a better understanding of a company's culture:

•   What are the company's core values?

•   How would you describe the company's work environment?

•   What opportunities are there for professional development and growth?

•   How does the company celebrate successes?

•   How does the company handle conflict or disagreements?

•   What's the company's approach to work-life balance?

Red Flags to Watch Out For

While there's no one-size-fits-all answer to what constitutes a good company culture, there are some red flags you should watchout for:

- **High turnover rate:** This could indicate that employees areunhappy and leaving in droves.

- **Negative reviews on Glassdoor or Indeed:** Take these reviews with a grain of salt, but if you see a pattern of complaints about the culture, it's worth investigating further.

- **A lack of diversity and inclusion:** A diverse workforce is a sign of a healthy and welcoming culture.

- **A toxic work environment:** If you get a sense that employees are stressed, overworked, or unhappy, it's probably not a place you want to work.

- **Misalignment of values:** If the company's values don't resonate with you, it's unlikely to be a good fit in the long run.

Trust Your Gut

Ultimately, the best way to assess a company's culture is to trust your gut. Pay attention to how you feel when you're interacting with the company's representatives. Do they seem genuine and enthusiastic? Do you feel like you could fit in with the team?

Remember, you're not just looking for a job; you're hiring your boss. Choose a company where you feel valued, supported, and inspired to do your best work.

By prioritizing cultural fit, you're not only setting yourself up for success in your new role, but you're also ensuring a fulfilling and enjoyable career journey. Don't settle for a job that doesn't align with who you are and what you value. Take the time to find a company where you can truly thrive.

Researching Potential Employers

You wouldn't buy a car without kicking the tires, checking under the hood, and taking it for a test drive, right? The same principle applies to choosing your next employer. Thorough research is essential to ensure you're not just landing a job, but hiring a boss and a company that aligns with your values, goals, and overall career vision.

Think of yourself as a detective, gathering clues to build a complete picture of your potential workplace. Here's your investigation toolkit:

1. The Company Website: Your Primary Source

The company website is your first stop. Pay close attention to their mission statement, values, and company culture pages. Look for clues about their work environment, employee testimonials, and any recent awards or recognition. If they have a blog or news section, read recent articles to get a feel for the company's voice and priorities.

2. LinkedIn: The Professional Network

LinkedIn is a treasure trove of information. Search for the company's profile and see how they present themselves. Check out employee profiles to get a sense of their backgrounds and career paths. Look for any shared connections who might be able to provide insider information. You can also join relevant LinkedIn groups to see what current and former employees are saying about the company.

3. Glassdoor and Other Review Sites: Unfiltered Opinions

While not always entirely accurate, employee reviews on sites like Glassdoor can offer valuable insights. Look for patterns in the feedback. Are employees generally happy? What are the pros and cons of working there? Pay attention to reviews about the company culture, work-life balance, and management style.

4. News and Press Releases: Staying Informed

Search for recent news articles and press releases about the company. This can reveal their latest projects, financial performance, and any significant changes or challenges they're facing. It's also a good way to gauge their reputation and public image.

5. Social Media: A Window into Culture

Check out the company's social media channels (Twitter, Facebook, Instagram, etc.). This can give you a glimpse into their culture, values, and how they interact with their audience. Look for posts about company events, employee spotlights, and social responsibility initiatives.

6. Competitors: Understanding the Landscape

Researching the company's competitors can provide valuable context. How do they compare in terms of size, market share, and reputation? What are their strengths and weaknesses? This can help you assess the company's position in the industry and its potential for growth.

7. Informational Interviews: The Inside Scoop

If possible, try to arrange informational interviews with current or former employees. This is your chance to ask questions about the company culture, the day-to-day work experience, and any other details you can't find online. Be sure to prepare thoughtful questions and approach these conversations with genuine curiosity.

Red Flags to Watch For

As you conduct your research, be on the lookout for potential red flags, such as:

- **High turnover rate:** If employees seem to come and go quickly, it could be a sign of a toxic work environment or poor management.

- **Negative press or reviews:** Multiple negative reviews or news articles could indicate deeper issues within the company.

- **Inconsistent messaging:** If the company's website, social media, and employee reviews paint vastly different pictures, it's worth investigating further.

- **Lack of transparency:** If it's difficult to find

information about the company or their leadership team, it could be a cause for concern.

Going Beyond the Surface

Don't stop at the obvious sources. Dig deeper to get a more nuanced understanding of the company. Here are some additionaltips:

- **Talk to your network:** Ask friends, colleagues, or former classmates if they have any insights or connections at the company.

- **Look for industry reports:** Check industry publications or analyst reports to see how the company is perceived within their sector.

- **Attend industry events:** If possible, attend conferences or networking events where the company may be present. This can give you a chance to observe their representativesand interact with them informally.

Documenting Your Findings

As you gather information, create a document to organize your findings. Note down key facts, observations, and any questions that arise. This will help you compare different companies and make an informed decision about where to apply.

The Power of Research

Thorough research is an investment in your career. It empowers you to make informed choices, avoid potential pitfalls, and ultimately, hire a boss and a company that aligns with your vision for success. Remember, you're not just looking for a job; you're building a career, and the foundation starts with the right employer.

Asking the Right Questions

The interview isn't just about them grilling you; it's a two-way street. You're not only showcasing your skills and experience but also assessing if this company is a place where you'll thrive. Asking the right questions is your secret weapon to uncover the company's culture, values, and how well they align with your own.

Why Questions Matter

Let's be honest, a company's website and marketing materials often paint a rosy picture. But what's the reality? Asking insightful questions helps you peek behind the curtain. It demonstrates your interest, preparation, and proactive nature, making you a more attractive candidate. More importantly, it gives you invaluable information to make an informed decision about your future.

Crafting Your Question Arsenal

Forget generic questions like, "What's the company culture like?" or "What are the growth opportunities?" Instead, craft questions that delve deeper, spark meaningful conversation, and reveal the company's true colors. Here are some powerful categories to focus on:

1. **Values and Mission:**

"How does the company's mission statement translate into daily work?"

"Can you share an example of a time the company's values were put into action?"

"What are some of the biggest challenges the company is facing in living its values?"

2. **Growth and Development:**

"What are the opportunities for professional development and growth within the company?"

"How does the company support employees in learning new skills and taking on new challenges?"

"Can you describe a recent example of how the company has invested in employee development?"

3. **Collaboration and Teamwork:**

"How would you describe the collaboration and teamwork culture here?"

"Can you share an example of a successful cross-functional project?"

"How are disagreements and conflicts handled within teams?"

4. **Work-Life Balance:**

"What does work-life balance look like at this company?"

"How does the company support employees in

maintaining a healthy work-life balance?"

"Are there any flexible work arrangements available?"

5. Leadership and Management:

"How would you describe the leadership style of the company's executives?"

"What qualities does the company look for in its managers?"

"Can you share an example of a time a manager went above and beyond to support their team?"

Tailoring Your Questions

Don't just blindly ask these questions. Tailor them to the specific company and role you're interviewing for. For example, if the company emphasizes innovation, ask about how they foster a culture of creativity. If the role requires strong teamwork, inquire about how collaboration is encouraged and rewarded.

Reading Between the Lines

Pay attention to the interviewer's body language, tone of voice, and the specifics of their answers. Are they enthusiastic and specific, or vague and hesitant? Do their answers align with what you've learned about the company from other sources? Your gut feeling is a powerful tool here.

Red Flags to Watch For

Be wary of answers that are overly generic, dismissive, or avoid the question altogether. If the interviewer seems uncomfortable or unable to answer your questions, it could be a sign that the company culture isn't what they claim it to be.

Beyond the Interview

Your quest for cultural alignment doesn't end with the interview. Talk to current or former employees, read online reviews, and observe the company's social media presence. These additional sources can provide valuable insights into the company's trueculture.

Remember:

The goal isn't to find a perfect company (they don't exist). It's to find a company where you feel valued, respected, and where your values align with theirs. By asking insightful questions, you'll gain the clarity you need to make a confident decision about your career.

Remember, this is just a starting point. Craft your own questions based on your priorities and values. With the right questions, you'll not only impress the interviewer but also gain valuable insights into whether this company is the right fit for you.

Your dream job is out there. Now go hire your boss!

Chapter 7: Networking with Purpose

Let's be honest – the word "networking" can evoke a mix of emotions. For some, it conjures images of awkward cocktail parties, forced conversations, and desperate attempts to hand out business cards. For others, it's a necessary evil, a chore to be endured in the pursuit of career advancement.

But what if I told you that networking doesn't have to be painful? In fact, it can be one of the most rewarding and enjoyable aspects of your job search.

Networking, when done right, is about building genuine relationships, fostering connections, and creating a supportive community that empowers you to achieve your goals. It's not about schmoozing or using people; it's about connecting with others on a human level, sharing your passions and aspirations, and finding common ground.

In this chapter, we're going to ditch the outdated notion of networking as a transactional exchange and embrace it as a powerful tool for building a fulfilling career. We'll explore how to:

- **Shift your mindset:** Move beyond the transactional approach and focus on building authentic relationships.

- **Identify your networking goals:** Determine what you want to achieve through networking and who can help you get there.

- **Expand your network strategically:** Connect

with people who share your interests, values, and career aspirations.

- **Make a lasting impression:** Craft a compelling personalbrand that reflects your unique value proposition.

- **Leverage online platforms:** Use LinkedIn and other social media to connect with potential employers and mentors.

- **Nurture your relationships:** Stay in touch with yournetwork and offer support whenever possible.

By the end of this chapter, you'll be equipped with the tools and strategies you need to network with confidence, authenticity, andpurpose. You'll learn how to turn networking from a dreaded task into a fulfilling activity that propels your career forward.

So, get ready to ditch the business cards, put away the elevator pitch, and start building meaningful connections that will last a lifetime. It's time to network with purpose.

Building Authentic Relationships

Networking. The word itself might conjure up images of awkward cocktail parties, forced conversations, and a relentless exchange ofbusiness cards. But what if I told you there's a better way—a way that focuses on genuine connections, mutual support, and long-term relationships?

In the "Hire Your Boss" framework, networking isn't about collecting contacts like trophies; it's about building a community of people who genuinely want to see you succeed. It's about giving as much as you receive, offering support, and fostering connections that go beyond the transactional.

Shifting Your Mindset

The first step to building authentic relationships is a mindset shift. Instead of viewing networking as a necessary evil, approach it as an opportunity to connect with interesting people, learn from their experiences, and expand your horizons.

Think of networking as a way to build your personal "board of directors"—a group of trusted advisors who can offer guidance, support, and insights as you navigate your career journey. As Herminia Ibarra, a renowned leadership expert, puts it, "Networking is not about collecting contacts; it's about planting relations."

Networking as a Two-Way Street

Remember, networking is a two-way street. It's not just about what others can do for you; it's about what you can offer them as well. Be generous with your time, expertise, and connections. Offer to help others in their job search, introduce them to relevant contacts, or share valuable information.

By approaching networking with a spirit of generosity, you'll not only build stronger relationships but also create a positive reputation for yourself. People are more likely to want to help someone who has been helpful to them.

Building Connections That Last

Building authentic relationships takes time and effort. It's not something you can do overnight. But the rewards are well worth it. When you have a strong network of genuine connections, you'llhave access to:

- **Job Leads:** Your network can be a valuable source of job leads that you might not find through traditional channels.

- **Mentorship:** Experienced professionals can offer guidance,advice, and support as you navigate your career.

- **Industry Insights:** Networking can help you stay up-to-date on industry trends, best practices, and new technologies.

- **Moral Support:** Your network can be a source of encouragement and support during challenging times.

Tips for Building Authentic Relationships

Here are some practical tips for building genuine connections:

1. **Focus on Quality Over Quantity:** It's better to have a few deep connections than a large number of superficial ones.

2. **Be Authentic:** Don't try to be someone you're not. Peopleare drawn to authenticity and sincerity.

3. **Listen More Than You Talk:** Ask thoughtful

questions andshow genuine interest in the other person.

4.   **Follow Up:** After meeting someone, send a thank-you noteor email and stay in touch periodically.

5.   **Give Back:** Offer to help others in any way you can. Be aresource and a support system.

Networking Beyond the Traditional

Networking doesn't just happen at formal events or conferences. You can build relationships through online platforms like LinkedIn, industry groups, or even volunteer organizations. The key is to be open to connecting with people from all walks of life.

Conclusion

Building authentic relationships is an essential part of the "Hire Your Boss" framework. By shifting your mindset, focusing on genuine connections, and approaching networking as a two-way street, you'll create a powerful network of support that can propel your career to new heights.

Remember, the most successful professionals aren't just good at their jobs; they're also good at building relationships. Invest in your network, and it will pay dividends for years to come.

Leveraging LinkedIn

If the "Hire Your Boss" framework is your career compass, LinkedIn is your digital map. It's where you showcase your professional brand, connect with potential employers, and discover hidden opportunities. But like any tool, it's only as powerful as the person wielding it. In this section, we'll dive into practical strategies for optimizing your LinkedIn profile and using it to network like a pro.

Crafting a Compelling Profile: Your Digital Resume

Your LinkedIn profile is more than just an online resume—it's your personal landing page, your virtual handshake with the professional world. Think of it as your opportunity to make a lasting first impression.

- **Professional Photo:** Ditch the selfie and invest in a high-quality headshot that exudes confidence and professionalism. A study by LinkedIn found that profiles with professional photos are 14 times more likely to be viewed.

- **Headline:** Don't just list your job title. Use this prime real estate to highlight your unique value proposition. Think of it as your professional tagline—what do you want people to know about you at a glance?

- **Summary:** This is your elevator pitch in written form. Tell your story, showcase your passions, and highlight your accomplishments. Use strong verbs and keywords that resonate with your target audience.

- **Experience:** Don't just copy and paste your resume. Use this section to elaborate on your achievements, quantify your results, and demonstrate your impact. Think of it as your opportunity to show, not just tell.

• **Skills and Endorsements:** Add relevant skills to your profile and encourage colleagues and connections to endorse you. This social proof can boost your credibility and visibility.

• **Recommendations:** Request recommendations from former supervisors, colleagues, or clients. These testimonials can add valuable third-party validation to your profile.

• **Featured Section:** Showcase your best work by adding links to articles, projects, or presentations. This is your chance to let your accomplishments speak for themselves.

Remember, your profile is a living document. Keep it updated with your latest projects, skills, and achievements. The more complete and engaging your profile, the more likely you are to attract the right opportunities.

Networking Like a Pro: Building Meaningful Connections

LinkedIn is a goldmine for networking, but it's not about amassing a huge number of connections. It's about building genuine relationships with people who can help you achieve your career goals.

• **Connect Strategically:** Start by connecting with people you know—former colleagues, classmates, mentors, and friends. Then, expand your network by joining groups relevant to your industry and interests.

• **Engage Authentically:** Don't just send generic connection requests. Personalize your messages, mention something you admire about their profile, or find a common interest to spark conversation.

• **Add Value:** Share insightful articles, comment on posts, and participate in discussions. Position yourself as a thought leader and contribute to the community.

• **Request Informational Interviews:** Reach out to people in your desired field and ask for informational interviews. This is a great way to learn more about their career path, gain insights, and expand your network.

• **Be Helpful:** Offer to help others in your network whenever possible. This could be as simple as sharing a job posting or making an introduction. Remember, networking is a two-way street.

By following these tips, you can turn LinkedIn into your personal networking powerhouse. You'll build a strong online presence, establish yourself as a thought leader, and open doors to new opportunities.

Finding Hidden Opportunities: The Job Search Secret Weapon

LinkedIn isn't just for networking; it's also a powerful job search tool. Here's how to use it to your advantage:

- **Job Search:** Use LinkedIn's job search function to find openings that match your skills and interests. Filter by location, industry, company size, and more.

- **Company Pages:** Follow companies you admire to stay up-to-date on their latest news and job postings. You can also see who you're connected to at the company, which can help you get your foot in the door.

- **Alumni Networks:** Connect with alumni from your school or former workplaces. They can provide valuable insights, leads, and even referrals.

- **LinkedIn Premium:** If you're serious about your job search, consider upgrading to LinkedIn Premium. It gives you access to additional features like InMail (direct messaging), salary insights, and more.

Remember, the job search is a process, not an event. Be patient, persistent, and proactive. By leveraging LinkedIn's powerful tools and resources, you'll increase your chances of landing your dream job.

In Conclusion

LinkedIn is a powerful tool that can help you achieve your career goals. By optimizing your profile, building meaningful connections, and actively searching for opportunities, you can leverage this platform to its full potential.

Remember, the "Hire Your Boss" mindset is all about

taking control of your career journey. LinkedIn is your digital ally in this endeavor. Use it wisely, and you'll be well on your way to hiring the boss you deserve.

Informational Interviews

Informational interviews might be the most underutilized tool in the job seeker's arsenal. They're not about asking for a job; they're about gaining invaluable insights into your desired industry, building relationships with people who work there, and ultimately, positioning yourself as a knowledgeable and engaged candidate.

What is an Informational Interview?

An informational interview is a casual conversation with someone working in a field or company that interests you. It's a chance to ask questions, learn about their career path, and get their perspective on the industry. Think of it as a fact-finding mission, not a job pitch.

Why Should You Conduct Informational Interviews?

1.   **Insider Knowledge:** You'll gain insights you won't find in job descriptions or company websites. You'll learn about the day-to-day realities of the job, the challenges and rewards, and the skills that are most valued.

2.   **Network Expansion:** You'll build relationships with people who can offer advice, introduce you to others in their network, and potentially even become advocates for

your career.

3. **Skill Development:** You'll practice your communication and interpersonal skills, which are essential for any job.

4. **Confidence Boost:** You'll gain a better understanding of theindustry and feel more confident in your job search.

5. **Hidden Opportunities:** Sometimes, informational interviews can even lead to unadvertised job openings.

How to Set Up an Informational Interview

1. **Identify Your Targets:** Think about people you know (or people you'd like to know) who work in your desired field. This could be former colleagues, alumni from your school, or connections you've made through LinkedIn.

2. **Reach Out:** Send a personalized email or LinkedIn messageexplaining who you are, why you're interested in their work, and what you hope to learn from the interview. Keepit brief and professional.

3. **Schedule a Time:** Be flexible and offer a few different time slots. Most informational interviews are conducted over the phone or video call, but in-person meetings are also possible.

4. **Prepare Your Questions:** Have a list of thoughtful questions ready. This will show you've done your research and are genuinely interested in their insights.

What Questions to Ask

- How did you get started in your career?

- What do you enjoy most about your job?

- What are the biggest challenges you face?

- What skills and qualities are most important for success in this field?

- What advice would you give to someone starting out inthis industry?

- Do you know anyone else I could talk to who might have similar insights?

Tips for a Successful Informational Interview

- **Be Respectful of Their Time:** Keep the interview to 30 minutes or less unless they offer to extend it.

- **Be Engaged and Curious:** Ask follow-up questions and show genuine interest in what they have to say.

- **Take Notes:** Jot down key takeaways and any names of other people they suggest you contact.

- **Follow Up:** Send a thank-you email within 24 hours. Mention something specific you learned from the interview and express your gratitude for their time.

Informational Interviews in the Age of LinkedIn

LinkedIn has revolutionized the way we network. It's a powerful tool for connecting with professionals in your field, and it can be a great way to set up informational interviews. Here's how:

1. **Optimize Your Profile:** Make sure your LinkedIn profile is up-to-date and highlights your skills and experience.

2. **Join Groups:** Join relevant LinkedIn groups and participate in discussions. This is a great way to make connections and get noticed.

3. **Request an Introduction:** If you have a mutual connection, ask them to introduce you to the person you want to interview.

4. **Send a Personalized Message:** If you don't have a mutual connection, send a personalized message explaining why you'd like to connect and schedule an informational interview.

Remember: Informational interviews are a two-way street. Offer to share your own experiences or insights if relevant. The goal is to build a relationship, not just extract information.

Case Study: Sarah's Success with Informational Interviews

Sarah, a recent college graduate, was struggling to break into the marketing industry. She had sent out countless resumes and cover letters but hadn't received any interviews. Then, she decided to try informational interviews.

Sarah reached out to alumni from her school who worked

in marketing and asked if they would be willing to chat with her. To her surprise, several people agreed. During these conversations, Sarah learned about the different roles in marketing, the skills that were most in demand, and the challenges and rewards of the industry. She also made valuable connections with people who were impressed by her initiative and enthusiasm.

After a few weeks of conducting informational interviews, Sarah was offered an interview for a marketing coordinator position at a leading tech company. She was well-prepared for the interview, thanks to the insights she had gained from her conversations. She was also able to reference her network of contacts, which demonstrated her commitment to the industry.

Sarah landed the job, and she credits her success to the power of informational interviews. "I wouldn't have gotten my foot in the door without them," she says. "They gave me the confidence and knowledge I needed to succeed." (Smith, 2023)

Your Turn

Now it's your turn to harness the power of informational interviews. Don't be afraid to reach out to people in your desired field and ask for their insights. You'll be surprised at how willing they are to help, and you might just learn something that changes the course of your career. Remember, the "Hire Your Boss" framework is all about taking control of your job search and positioning yourself for success. Informational interviews are a powerful tool in your arsenal. Use them wisely, and you'll be well on your way to landing your dream job.

Chapter 8: Mastering the Interview Process

Congratulations! You've made it to the interview stage. You've nailed your positioning, found companies that align with yourvalues, and now it's time to seal the deal. But let's be honest, interviews can be nerve-wracking. Sweaty palms, racing heart, the fear of saying the wrong thing – we've all been there.

The good news is, interviews don't have to be a source of anxiety. In fact, with the right preparation and mindset, they can be an exciting opportunity to showcase your skills, connect with potential employers, and ultimately, land your dream job.

In this chapter, we're going to demystify the interview process and equip you with practical strategies to shine. We'll cover everything from pre-interview research to answering those dreaded behavioral questions with confidence and finesse.

No more stumbling through answers or second-guessing yourself. By the end of this chapter, you'll be armed with the tools and techniques to walk into any interview room feeling calm, collected, and ready to impress.

Remember, this isn't just about getting the job – it's about finding the right job, the one where you can truly thrive and make a meaningful contribution. So, let's dive in and prepare you to ace your next interview and "hire your boss" with confidence!

Preparation is Key

The job interview isn't just a Q&A session; it's your grand finale, the culmination of your Hire Your Boss journey. It's your chance to shine, to demonstrate your value, and to ultimately, secure the jobof your dreams. But don't be fooled – winging it won't cut it. This is where your preparation, guided by Clarity, Positioning, and Alignment, truly pays off.

Clarity: Know Thyself, Know Thy Goal

Before you step into that interview room (or log into that Zoom call), you need unwavering clarity on three key aspects:

1.   **Your Career Vision:** Revisit your career vision statement. What are your long-term goals? What kind of impact do you want to make? This clarity will infuse your answers with passion and purpose.

2.   **Your Unique Value Proposition:** What sets you apart from other candidates? What specific skills and experiences can you offer the company? This understanding will help you articulate your value proposition with confidence.

3.   **Your Ideal Work Environment:** What kind of company culture do you thrive in? What type of boss do you want to work for? This knowledge will guide your questions and help you assess if the company is the right fit.

Remember, clarity breeds confidence. The more you know yourself and your goals, the more persuasive and authentic you'll be in the interview.

Positioning: Crafting Your Narrative

Think of your interview as a storytelling session. You're the protagonist, and your career is the story. But like any good story, it needs a structure, a narrative arc that captivates the audience (aka, your interviewer).

Start by identifying key moments in your career – your accomplishments, challenges you've overcome, and lessons you've learned. These are the building blocks of your story. Then, weave them into a cohesive narrative that showcases your skills, your growth, and your potential.

To make your story even more compelling, use the STAR method (Situation, Task, Action, Result) to answer behavioral interview questions. This method provides a clear and concise way to illustrate your skills and experiences with real-world examples.

For instance, if asked about a time you faced a challenge, don't just say, "I'm a great problem solver." Instead, describe a specific situation where you encountered a challenge, explain the task you were responsible for, detail the actions you took to overcome the challenge, and highlight the positive results you achieved.

Remember, your story is your superpower. Use it to

position yourself as the ideal candidate for the job.

Alignment: Finding the Right Fit

An interview is a two-way street. It's not just about the company evaluating you; it's also about you evaluating the company. Does their culture align with your values? Does their vision resonate with your goals?

To ensure alignment, do your homework. Research the company thoroughly. Read their website, their social media, and any articles or reviews you can find. Talk to current or former employees if possible. This will give you valuable insights into the company's culture and values.

During the interview, ask insightful questions that reveal the company's culture and values. For example, you could ask:

- What are the company's core values?

- How does the company promote work-life balance?

- What opportunities are there for professional development?

Your questions will not only help you assess if the company is the right fit, but they'll also demonstrate your genuine interest in the opportunity.

The "Hire Your Boss" Interview Prep Checklist

To help you prepare for your interview, I've created a

handy checklist:

- **Review the job description:** Identify the key skills and qualifications required for the role.

- **Research the company:** Learn about their products, services, mission, and values.

- **Prepare your STAR stories:** Identify specific examples from your career that demonstrate your skills and accomplishments.

- **Practice your answers:** Role-play with a friend or family member to refine your responses.

- **Prepare your questions:** Come up with insightful questions that reveal the company's culture and values.

- **Dress professionally:** Make a good first impression with your attire.

- **Arrive early:** Show respect for the interviewer's time.

- **Be confident:** Project confidence in your abilities and your value.

By following this checklist and leveraging the power of Clarity, Positioning, and Alignment, you'll be well-prepared to ace your interview and hire the boss you deserve.

Storytelling for Impact

Let's face it: no one likes a boring interview. A monotonous recitation of your resume won't captivate your potential boss. But what will? Stories. Compelling narratives that showcase your skills, experiences, and the unique value you bring to the table.

Think of your interview as a stage, and you're the protagonist. Your goal is to engage your audience (the interviewer), evoke emotions, and leave a lasting impression. And the most effective way to do that is through storytelling.

Why Stories Matter

Stories are powerful tools for communication. They tap into our emotions, making information more memorable and relatable. When you tell a story, you're not just listing facts and figures; you're transporting your listener into a specific moment in time, allowing them to experience it alongside you.

In an interview setting, stories can:

• **Demonstrate your skills in action:** Instead of just saying you're a "problem solver," tell a story about a time you successfully tackled a complex challenge.

• **Highlight your impact:** Quantify your accomplishments by weaving numbers and results into your narratives.

• **Reveal your personality and values:** Let your authentic self shine through your stories, giving the interviewer a glimpse of who you are as a person.

• **Create a connection:** Stories have a way of forging connections between people. By sharing your experiences, you can build rapport with the interviewer and leave a positive impression."

The STAR Method: Your Storytelling Framework

To craft impactful stories, follow the STAR method:

1. **Situation:** Set the scene by describing the context of your story. What was the challenge or opportunity you faced?

2. **Task:** Explain your specific role or responsibility in the situation. What were you tasked with doing?

3. **Action:** Describe the actions you took to address the situation. What steps did you take, and what skills did you utilize?

4. **Result:** Share the outcome of your actions. What were the results or achievements? Quantify your impact whenever possible.

Example: Demonstrating Problem-Solving Skills

Situation: "At my previous company, we were facing a major issue with customer churn. We were losing customers at an alarming rate, and it was impacting our bottom line."

Task: "As the marketing manager, I was tasked with identifying the root causes of the churn and developing a strategy to address it."

Action: "I conducted extensive customer surveys, analyzed data, and collaborated with our customer service team to gather insights. Based on my findings, I developed a comprehensive customer retention plan that included targeted email campaigns, personalized offers, and loyalty programs."

Result: "Within six months of implementing the plan, we saw a 25% reduction in customer churn, which resulted in a significant increase in revenue. We also received positive feedback from customers who felt more valued and appreciated."

Tips for Effective Storytelling

- **Keep it concise:** Don't ramble. Get to the point and highlight the most relevant details.

- **Use vivid language:** Paint a picture with your words and use sensory details to engage the listener.

- **Focus on the positive:** Even if the outcome wasn't perfect, frame your story in a positive light, highlighting what you learned or how you grew.

- **Practice, practice, practice:** Rehearse your stories until youcan tell them naturally and confidently.

- **Be authentic:** Don't try to be someone you're not. Let yourpersonality shine through.

Tailoring Your Stories

It's important to tailor your stories to the specific job

you're applying for. Research the company's values and the job description, and choose stories that highlight skills and experiences relevant to the role.

For example, if you're interviewing for a leadership position, share stories that demonstrate your ability to motivate and inspire others. If you're applying for a technical role, focus on stories that showcase your problem-solving and analytical skills.

References and Further Reading

To delve deeper into the art of storytelling, consider these resources:

• Miller, Carmine Gallo. *The Storyteller's Secret: From TED Speakers to Business Legends, Why Some Ideas Catch On and Others Don't*. St. Martin's Press, 2016.

• Duarte, Nancy. *Resonate: Present Visual Stories that Transform Audiences*. John Wiley & Sons, 2010.

By mastering the art of storytelling, you'll transform your interviews into engaging conversations that showcase your value and leave a lasting impression. Remember, you're not just an applicant; you're a storyteller, a problem solver, and a potential asset to the company. Let your stories speak for themselves and pave the way to your dream job.

Behavioral Interview Questions

"Tell me about a time when..." If you've ever interviewed for a job, you've probably heard this phrase more times than you can count.

That's because behavioral interview questions are a staple of modern hiring practices. These questions are designed to delve into your past experiences to predict your future performance. They ask you to share specific examples of how you've handled challenges, demonstrated skills, and achieved results.

While behavioral questions can seem daunting, they're actually a golden opportunity to showcase your abilities and prove that you're the right fit for the job. By understanding the purpose of these questions and mastering a few key strategies, you can confidently navigate any behavioral interview and impress your potential employer.

Why Behavioral Questions Matter

Behavioral questions are based on the premise that past behavior is the best predictor of future behavior. By asking you to share real-life examples, interviewers can gain insights into your problem-solving skills, communication style, teamwork abilities, leadership potential, and adaptability.

Unlike traditional interview questions that focus on hypothetical scenarios ("What would you do if..."), behavioral questions force you to draw on your actual experiences. This makes it harder to provide canned responses or rely on generic answers. It also gives the interviewer a more accurate picture of your capabilities.

The STAR Method: Your Secret Weapon

The most effective way to answer behavioral interview questions is to use the STAR method. This acronym stands for:

- **Situation:** Describe the specific context or situation you were in.

- **Task:** Explain the task or challenge you faced.

- **Action:** Detail the actions you took to address the situationor overcome the challenge.

- **Result:** Share the positive outcomes or results you achieved.

By structuring your response using the STAR method, you ensure that your answer is clear, concise, and impactful. It also helps you avoid rambling or getting sidetracked.

Common Behavioral Interview Questions and How to Answer Them

Let's take a look at some common behavioral interview questions and how you can answer them using the STAR method:

Question 1: Tell me about a time when you faced a difficult challenge at work. How did you handle it?

- **Situation:** "In my previous role as a marketing manager, I was tasked with increasing website traffic by 20% within three months."

- **Task:** "This was a significant challenge, as our website traffic had been stagnant for some time."

- **Action:** "I conducted a thorough analysis of our website analytics, identified areas for improvement, and developed a comprehensive marketing strategy that included SEO optimization, content marketing, and social media campaigns."

- **Result:** "As a result of my efforts, website traffic increased by 25% within the given timeframe, exceeding our initial goal."

Question 2: Give me an example of a time when you had to work effectively with a team to achieve a common goal.

- **Situation:** "During a recent project, my team was responsible for launching a new product line within a tight deadline."

- **Task:** "We faced several obstacles, including resource constraints and conflicting priorities."

- **Action:** "I facilitated regular team meetings to ensure everyone was aligned, delegated tasks based on individual strengths, and maintained open communication throughout the project."

- **Result:** "Through effective teamwork and collaboration, we successfully launched the product line on time and received positive feedback from customers and stakeholders."

Question 3: Describe a time when you took initiative and went above and beyond your normal responsibilities.

- **Situation:** "While working as a customer service representative, I noticed a recurring issue with our product that was causing frustration for customers."

- **Task:** "I decided to take initiative and investigate the issue further."

- **Action:** "I conducted thorough research, gathered customer feedback, and presented my findings to my manager along with a proposed solution."

- **Result:** "My manager was impressed with my initiative and implemented my suggestions, which led to a significant decrease in customer complaints and an overall improvement in customer satisfaction."

Tips for Answering Behavioral Interview Questions

- **Be Specific:** Don't provide vague or generic answers. Use specific details and examples to illustrate your points.

- **Focus on Your Role:** When describing a team effort, highlight your specific contributions and the actions you took.

- **Quantify Your Results:** Whenever possible, use

numbers and metrics to demonstrate the impact of your actions.

- **Be Honest and Authentic:** Don't exaggerate or fabricate stories. Be genuine and let your personality shine through.

Preparing for Behavioral Interviews

The best way to prepare for behavioral interviews is to brainstorm examples of past experiences that demonstrate the skills and qualities the employer is looking for. Review the job description and identify the key competencies required for the role. Then, think of specific instances where you've demonstrated those competencies.

Practice Makes Perfect

Once you have a few examples in mind, practice answering common behavioral interview questions using the STAR method. You can do this by yourself, with a friend or family member, or with a career counselor. The more you practice, the more confident and comfortable you'll become. (Yate, 2012)

The Bottom Line

Behavioral interview questions are an essential part of the modern hiring process. By understanding the purpose of these questions, mastering the STAR method, and preparing thoughtful responses, you can ace your next behavioral interview and land your dream job. Remember, your past experiences are a valuable asset – use them to your advantage!

Chapter 9: Negotiation Tactics for Job Seekers

Congratulations! You've nailed the interview, showcased your value, and impressed the hiring manager. But your job search journey isn't quite over yet. In fact, one of the most critical phasesis just beginning: negotiation.

Think of it like this: you've just been offered a starring role in a movie, but you still need to finalize your contract. The terms of that contract – your salary, benefits, vacation time, and even your job title – can significantly impact your overall satisfaction and financial well-being.

Unfortunately, many job seekers shy away from negotiation, fearing they'll jeopardize the offer or appear greedy. However, avoiding negotiation can be a costly mistake. By not advocating for yourself, you could be leaving thousands of dollars on the table each year.

In this chapter, we'll debunk common negotiation myths, equip you with powerful strategies, and guide you through the entire negotiation process. You'll learn how to:

- **Know your worth:** Research salary ranges, benefits packages, and industry standards to determine your market value.

- **Make the first move:** Don't wait for the employer to initiate the conversation – be proactive and confident in your ask.

- **Negotiate strategically:** Use a combination of data, persuasion, and compromise to reach a mutually beneficialagreement.

- **Go beyond salary:** Don't forget to negotiate other aspects of the job offer, such as benefits, vacation time, and professional development opportunities.

By mastering the art of negotiation, you'll not only maximize your compensation but also demonstrate your confidence, professionalism, and commitment to your career. Remember, thisisn't about being greedy; it's about advocating for your value and ensuring that you're fairly compensated for your skills and contributions.

So, let's dive in and discover how to negotiate like a pro, ensuring you land a job offer that not only excites you but also reflects yourtrue worth. After all, you've earned it.

Know Your Worth

Let's talk money. It's a topic that often makes people squirm, but in the job search, it's crucial to know your worth. After all, you're not just looking for a job; you're hiring your boss, and part of that is ensuring fair compensation for your skills and experience.

Why Research is Key

Going into salary negotiations blind is like walking into a store without knowing the prices. You wouldn't buy a car without researching its value, would you? The same principle applies to your career. Understanding the typical salary range for your desired position empowers you to negotiate confidently and secure a compensation package that reflects your true value.

Unearthing the Numbers

So, where do you start? Thankfully, we live in the age of information, and there are numerous resources available to help you determine your worth:

1. **Online Salary Calculators:** Websites like Glassdoor, Indeed, Salary.com, and PayScale offer salary calculators that allow you to input your job title, location, experience level, and other factors to get an estimated salary range. While these tools provide a good starting point, remember that they offer averages, and your actual salary may vary based on your specific skills and the company's compensation philosophy. (Glassdoor, n.d.; Indeed, n.d.; Salary.com, n.d.;PayScale, n.d.)

2. **Industry Reports:** Many industries have organizations or publications that release salary surveys and reports. These reports often provide more detailed information on salary ranges based on factors like company size, industry sector,and specific job responsibilities. Look for reputable sources like professional associations, industry publications, or consulting firms specializing in compensation data.(Bureau of Labor Statistics, 2023)

3. **Networking:** Talk to people in your field, especially those in similar roles or at companies you're targeting. They can provide valuable insights into salary expectations and negotiation tactics. Attend industry events or join online forums to connect with professionals and gather information.

4. **Professional Recruiters:** If you're working with a recruiter, they can also be a valuable resource for salary information. They have access to data from multiple companies and canoffer insights into current market trends.

Beyond Salary: Evaluating Benefits

Salary is just one piece of the compensation puzzle. Don't forget to factor in benefits when assessing a job offer. This includes:

• **Health Insurance:** Look at the cost of premiums, deductibles, and out-of-pocket maximums. Consider what type of coverage is offered (PPO, HMO, etc.) and whether it includes dental and vision.

• **Retirement Plans:** Does the company offer a 401(k) or other retirement plan? Do they match your contributions? What are the vesting schedules?

• **Paid Time Off (PTO):** How many days of vacation, sickleave, and personal days are you entitled to? Are there anyadditional paid holidays?

• **Other Perks:** Some companies offer additional

perks like tuition reimbursement, professional development opportunities, flexible work arrangements, or even on-site amenities like gyms or childcare.

Negotiating with Confidence

Once you have a clear understanding of your worth, it's time to negotiate. Remember, negotiation is not a confrontation; it's a conversation. Approach it with confidence, professionalism, and a willingness to compromise.

Here are some tips for successful salary negotiation:

• **Start with a Range:** Rather than stating a specific number, provide a salary range based on your research. This gives you some flexibility and demonstrates that you've done your homework.

• **Focus on Value:** Highlight your unique skills, experiences, and accomplishments. Explain how you can contribute to the company's success and why you're worth the investment.

• **Be Prepared to Counter:** If the initial offer is below your expectations, don't be afraid to counter. Be prepared with a well-reasoned justification for your counteroffer.

• **Consider the Total Package:** Don't just focus on salary. Negotiate for other benefits that are important to you, such as additional PTO, flexible work arrangements, or professional development opportunities.

Remember, the "Hire Your Boss" mindset is about empowerment. By knowing your worth and negotiating confidently, you're not just securing a paycheck; you're investing in your career and your future.

Negotiating Confidently

Congratulations! You've landed a job offer. This is a major accomplishment, but it's not the end of the road. In fact, it's the beginning of a crucial negotiation phase where you can potentially secure a compensation package that truly reflects your value. Negotiating might seem daunting, but with the right approach and mindset, you can confidently advocate for your worth and secure a deal that aligns with your career goals.

Know Your Worth: The Foundation of Confidence

Before you even step into a negotiation, it's essential to arm yourself with knowledge. Research the typical salary range for your position, industry, and experience level. Websites like Glassdoor, Indeed, and Salary.com can provide valuable insights. Talk to colleagues, mentors, or recruiters to get a sense of what others in similar roles are earning.

"Knowing your worth is not just about salary; it's about understanding the full value you bring to the table," says negotiation expert Linda Babcock.[1] This includes your skills, experience, education, and any unique attributes that set you apart. Quantify your achievements whenever possible. Did you increase sales by a certain percentage? Did you streamline a process that saved the company money? These are powerful data points to leverage during negotiations.

Strategies for Negotiating Salary

When it comes to salary negotiation, there are several effectivestrategies you can employ:

1.   **Aim High:** Don't be afraid to ask for more than the initial offer. Most employers expect some negotiation, and starting high gives you room to maneuver.

2.   **Justify Your Ask:** Back up your request with concrete evidence of your value. Highlight your achievements, skills, and experience. If you've done your research, you can alsocite industry salary data to support your position.

3.   **Be Prepared to Counter:** If the employer counters your initial offer, be prepared with a well-reasoned response. You can point to additional skills or experiences that justify your higher salary.

4.   **Focus on the Value You Bring:** Frame your negotiation in terms of the value you'll bring to the company. Explain how your skills and expertise will help the company achieve its goals and generate revenue.

5.   **Don't Rush:** Take your time to consider the offer

before accepting. If you need more time to think it over, politely ask for it.

Negotiating Beyond Salary: Benefits and Perks

Salary is just one piece of the compensation puzzle. Don't forget to negotiate other aspects of the package, such as:

• **Sign-on Bonus:** If you're leaving another job or relocating for this position, a sign-on bonus can help offset your costs.

• **Paid Time Off (PTO):** Many companies offer a standard amount of PTO, but you can often negotiate for additional vacation days or personal days.

• **Health Insurance:** Inquire about the details of the company's health insurance plan and whether there are options to upgrade coverage.

• **Retirement Contributions:** If the company offers a 401(k) or similar plan, negotiate for a higher employer match or contribution.

• **Professional Development:** Ask about opportunities for training, conferences, or certifications that can help you advance your career.

• **Flexible Work Arrangements:** If you're looking for flexibility in your schedule or the ability to work remotely, don't hesitate to bring it up. Many companies are open to these arrangements, especially in today's work environment.

Navigating the Negotiation Process

Negotiation is a dance, not a battle. It's about finding a mutually beneficial agreement that leaves both you and the employer satisfied. Here are some tips for navigating the process:

- **Be Professional:** Maintain a positive and respectful tonethroughout the negotiation.

- **Be Confident:** Believe in your worth and don't be afraid toask for what you deserve.

- **Be Prepared:** Do your research, practice your pitch, andanticipate potential counterarguments.

- **Be Flexible:** Be willing to compromise on some points, butdon't give away too much too soon.

The Power of Confidence

Negotiation is as much about mindset as it is about tactics. If you believe in your value and approach the negotiation with confidence, you're more likely to achieve a favorable outcome. Remember, you're not just asking for a favor; you're negotiating a business deal based on your skills and experience.

"The most important thing is to be prepared and to know what you want," advises negotiation expert Deepak Malhotra.[2] "If you're clear about your goals and you're confident in your abilities, you're more likely to get what you're after."

By following these strategies and embracing a confident mindset, you can transform job offers into dream deals that align with your career aspirations and financial goals. Remember, the "Hire Your Boss" framework empowers you to take control of your career destiny.

Navigating Counteroffers

So, you've landed a job offer. Congratulations! But hold on – your current employer just threw a curveball: a counteroffer. Suddenly,the path forward isn't so clear. Should you stay for the raise and perks, or stick with your decision to move on?

Navigating counteroffers can feel like walking a tightrope. There's the thrill of recognition, the tempting promise of improved conditions, and the underlying question of whether the grass is truly greener on the other side.

Let's break down this complex scenario and equip you with the tools to make an informed decision.

Understanding the Psychology of Counteroffers

First, it's crucial to understand why companies make counteroffers. It's often less about your irreplaceability and more about mitigating the disruption and cost of replacing you.

"Counteroffers are often motivated by the company's

desire to retain a valuable employee and avoid the time, expense, and uncertainty of finding a replacement," says career coach Sarah Jensen (2023).

Consider these common motivations behind counteroffers:

- **Preventing disruption:** Your departure could leave a holein projects or team dynamics.

- **Avoiding recruitment costs:** Hiring and onboarding a new employee can be expensive.

- **Protecting institutional knowledge:** You might possess valuable insights and expertise that are hard to replace.

Remember, a counteroffer doesn't always equate to newfound appreciation. It's a business decision, not necessarily a personal one.

Evaluating the Counteroffer: Key Considerations

Before you jump to conclusions, carefully evaluate the counteroffer. Ask yourself these critical questions:

1. **Is it just about money?** If the only change is a higher salary or better benefits, will that truly address the reasons you wanted to leave in the first place? Consider factors like career growth, work-life balance, company culture, andyour relationship with your manager.

2. **Are the changes sustainable?** Are the promises

made in the counteroffer realistic and feasible in the long run? Will your manager truly support your development, or was thisjust a knee-jerk reaction to your resignation?

3. **What message does it send?** Accepting a counteroffer could signal to your employer that you're primarily motivated by money, potentially impacting your future career prospects within the company.

4. **How does it compare to the new offer?** Evaluate both offers side-by-side, taking into account salary, benefits, career advancement opportunities, and cultural fit. Which option aligns better with your long-term goals and values?

Talking to Your (Potential) New Boss

It's also essential to consider the perspective of your potential new employer. Be transparent and communicate with them about the counteroffer. They might be willing to match or even exceed it, especially if they value your skills and experience.

"Open communication with the new employer can lead to a better understanding of their commitment to you and potentially a more favorable offer," suggests career advisor Michael Johnson (2022).

Trust Your Gut, But Weigh the Facts

Ultimately, the decision rests with you. Trust your instincts, but also carefully weigh the pros and cons of each option.

If the counteroffer genuinely addresses the underlying issues that led you to seek a new job, and you feel valued and appreciated, staying might be a good choice. However, if it's merely a band-aid solution or you have lingering doubts, moving on could be the better path for your career growth and overall satisfaction.

Additional Considerations:

- **Your reputation:** Be professional and respectful throughout the process, regardless of your decision. Burning bridges is never a good career move.

- **Long-term impact:** Consider how each choice will affect your long-term career goals and aspirations. Don't sacrifice your future for short-term gains.

- **Seek advice:** Talk to trusted mentors, career coaches, or friends for objective perspectives.

Remember, a counteroffer is an opportunity for reflection and reassessment. By carefully considering your options and prioritizing your long-term goals, you can make the best decision for your career.

Part III: Taking Action and Beyond

Chapter 10: Leveraging Online Platforms

Remember the days of printing out dozens of resumes, mailing them out, and hoping for the best? Thankfully, those days are long gone. In today's job market, your online presence isn't just an afterthought – it's your digital storefront, your personal billboard, your 24/7 networking hub.

Think about it: before a hiring manager even glances at your resume, they're likely to Google your name, check out your LinkedIn profile, and maybe even peek at your Twitter feed. What they find there can make or break your chances of landing an interview.

This chapter is your guide to building a powerful online presence that not only complements your "Hire Your Boss" strategy but amplifies it. We'll delve into the concrete steps you can take to:

• **Optimize Your LinkedIn Profile:** Turn it into a magnet for recruiters and showcase your professional brand.

• **Conquer Job Boards and Niche Sites:** Learn how to cut through the noise and find hidden opportunities.

• **Craft a Compelling Personal Website or Portfolio:** Make a lasting impression with a digital space that reflects your unique skills and experience.

This isn't about creating a fake persona or becoming an influencer overnight. It's about strategically leveraging online platforms to showcase your authentic self, connect with the right people, and open doors you might not have even known existed.

By the end of this chapter, you'll be armed with the knowledge and tools to make the internet work for you, not against you. You'll be well on your way to becoming a digital job search ninja, attracting opportunities like a magnet.

So, are you ready to build a digital footprint that screams "hire me"? Let's get started.

Optimizing Your Online Presence

Your online presence isn't just a collection of profiles; it's your digital brand. It's how potential employers, colleagues, and collaborators perceive you in the virtual realm. In today's interconnected world, a strong online presence can make or break your career opportunities. Think of it as your 24/7 resume, constantly working for you, even while you sleep.

Building a professional online brand isn't about vanity; it's about strategic visibility. It's about showcasing your expertise, connecting with the right people, and positioning yourself as the go-to person in your field.

In this section, we'll focus on LinkedIn, the undisputed king of professional networking, and explore how to optimize your presence on other relevant platforms.

LinkedIn: Your Digital Business Card

LinkedIn is your virtual handshake, your first impression

in the professional world. A well-crafted LinkedIn profile is your opportunity to tell your story, showcase your accomplishments, and connect with industry leaders. Here's how to make it shine:

1.   **Profile Picture:** Your profile picture is the visual anchor of your brand. Choose a professional headshot that's well-lit, friendly, and approachable. Avoid selfies, group photos, or anything too casual.

2.   **Headline:** Your headline is your virtual elevator pitch. Instead of simply stating your current job title, use this space to highlight your unique value proposition. For example, instead of "Marketing Manager," try "Results-Driven Marketing Strategist | Driving Growth Through Data & Creativity."

3.   **Summary:** Your summary is your chance to tell your story. Don't just list your skills; weave them into a narrative that showcases your personality, passion, and achievements. Use keywords relevant to your field to enhance your visibility in search results.

4.   **Experience:** Your experience section should be more than a chronological list of past jobs. Use action verbs to highlight your accomplishments, quantifying results whenever possible. For example, instead of "Managed social media accounts," write "Increased social media engagement by 35% through targeted campaigns and creative content."

5.   **Skills & Endorsements:** LinkedIn's skills section is

a valuable tool for showcasing your expertise. Choose relevant skills and encourage colleagues and connections to endorse you. This adds credibility to your profile.

6. **Recommendations:** Recommendations are like testimonials for your digital brand. Reach out to former colleagues, managers, or clients and ask them to write a recommendation highlighting your skills and contributions.

7. **Activity:** Don't be a passive observer on LinkedIn. Share relevant articles, comment on posts, and participate in group discussions. This shows you're engaged in your industry and keeps you top-of-mind with your network.

Beyond LinkedIn: Expanding Your Reach

While LinkedIn is essential, don't overlook other platforms where your target audience may be active. Consider creating a professional website or portfolio to showcase your work, contributing to industry blogs or publications, or participating in relevant online communities.

Remember, consistency is key. Ensure your messaging and branding are consistent across all platforms. This helps reinforce your professional identity and makes you more memorable.

Building Your Network: Connecting with Purpose

Networking isn't about collecting contacts; it's about building relationships. Focus on connecting with people who can help you learn, grow, and achieve your career goals. Reach out to colleagues, alumni, and industry leaders. Attend conferences and networking events (virtual or in-person). Don't be afraid to ask for informational interviews or career advice.

Remember, networking is a two-way street. Offer your expertise and support to others, and they'll be more likely to reciprocate.

The Power of Content: Sharing Your Expertise

One of the most effective ways to build your online brand is by sharing your knowledge and insights. Write blog posts, create videos, or participate in podcasts. Share your perspectives on industry trends, offer tips and advice, or showcase your work. By providing value to others, you establish yourself as a thought leader and attract opportunities.

By optimizing your online presence, building your network, and sharing your expertise, you'll create a powerful digital brand that opens doors and propels your career forward. Remember, your online presence is your 24/7 advocate. Invest in it wisely, and it will pay dividends in the long run.

Job Boards and Niche Sites

In the digital age, the job search has transformed into a

dynamic online landscape, and job boards and niche sites are your treasure maps to navigate this vast territory. They are the modern-day equivalent of bustling job fairs, offering a wealth of opportunities at your fingertips. But, like any treasure hunt, knowing where to look and how to search is key to unearthing the hidden gems.

Mastering the Mainstream Job Boards

The big players like Indeed, LinkedIn, Glassdoor, and Monster are your go-to resources for casting a wide net. These platforms aggregate job postings from various sources, giving you a comprehensive view of the job market.

- **Keyword Optimization:** Think like a recruiter. What keywords would they use to find someone like you? Sprinkle those keywords throughout your resume and profile to increase your visibility in search results.

- **Tailored Applications:** Resist the urge to blast out generic applications. Take the time to customize your resume and cover letter for each job, highlighting the skills and experiences that align with the specific requirements. (Smith 2023)

- **Job Alerts:** Set up job alerts to receive notifications when new positions matching your criteria are posted. This keeps you in the loop and allows you to apply quickly.

- **Beyond the Obvious:** Explore the additional features these platforms offer. LinkedIn, for instance, is a networking powerhouse. Connect with professionals in your field, join relevant groups, and participate in discussions to expand your reach.

Unveiling the Power of Niche Sites

While mainstream job boards offer a broad spectrum of opportunities, niche sites cater to specific industries or professions. These hidden gems can be invaluable for uncovering targeted openings that might not appear on larger platforms.

- **Industry-Specific Platforms:** Whether you're a software developer, healthcare professional, or marketing guru, there's a niche site tailored to your field. (Lee 2022)

- **Professional Associations:** Many professional organizations have job boards exclusive to their members. Consider joining these associations to access these hidden opportunities.

- **Company Career Pages:** Don't overlook the career pages of your target companies. Often, they list openings not advertised elsewhere.

Navigating the Digital Landscape

- **Organized Approach:** Create a system for tracking your applications, interviews, and follow-ups. A spreadsheet or online tool can help you stay organized and avoid missing any opportunities.

- **Be Authentic:** Let your personality shine through

in your online profiles and applications. Companies are looking forgenuine individuals who are passionate about their work. (Brown 2021)

- **Stay Persistent:** The job search can be a marathon, not a sprint. Don't get discouraged by rejections. Keep refining your approach, learning from your experiences, and persisting in your pursuit.

Example: A Tale of Two Job Seekers

Consider Sarah, a marketing professional with a passion for sustainable brands. While she found some relevant openings on mainstream job boards, her breakthrough came when she discovered a niche site dedicated to eco-conscious businesses. This led her to a dream role at a company perfectly aligned with her values.

On the other hand, Alex, a software engineer, leveraged LinkedIn to connect with recruiters at his target companies. His active participation in online discussions and insightful comments onindustry articles caught the attention of a hiring manager, leading to an interview and ultimately a job offer.

The Bottom Line

Job boards and niche sites are powerful tools, but they require a strategic approach. By understanding how to use them effectively,you can unlock a wealth of opportunities and "hire your boss" on your own terms. Remember, the job search is a journey of discovery, and these digital platforms are your trusty companions along the way.

Personal Website or Portfolio

In today's digital age, having a strong online presence is non-negotiable. It's your virtual handshake, your first impression, and a crucial tool for showcasing your skills and experience to potential employers. Think of it as your personal billboard, broadcasting your professional brand 24/7.

But don't worry, you don't need to be a tech whiz to create an impressive online portfolio. In this section, we'll guide you through the process step-by-step, offering practical advice and resources to help you build a digital showcase that truly represents your unique value proposition.

Why You Need a Personal Website or Portfolio

Before we dive into the how-to, let's talk about the why. Why should you invest time and effort in creating a personal website orportfolio?

1.   **Credibility:** A well-crafted online presence instantly boosts your credibility and professionalism. It shows you're serious about your career and willing to go the extra mile.

2.   **Control Your Narrative:** Your website or portfolio allows you to tell your story on your own terms. You can highlight your most relevant skills, experiences, and accomplishments, creating a narrative that resonates with

potential employers.

3.   **Stand Out from the Crowd:** In a sea of resumes, a personalwebsite or portfolio can help you stand out and leave a lasting impression. It's a chance to showcase your personality, creativity, and passion for your work.

4.   **Accessibility:** Unlike a traditional resume, your online portfolio is accessible to anyone, anywhere, at any time. This means more opportunities for your work to be seen and appreciated.

Choosing Your Platform

The first step is deciding whether to create a personal website or a portfolio. Both have their advantages and disadvantages, and the right choice for you depends on your specific needs and goals.

•   **Personal Website:** Offers more flexibility and customization options. You can create multiple pages, add a blog, and showcase a wider range of skills and experiences. However, it requires more technical know-how and time to set up and maintain.

•   **Portfolio:** A simpler option focused on showcasing your work visually. It's ideal for creatives like designers, photographers, and writers. Many user-friendly platforms make creating a stunning portfolio a breeze.

If you're unsure which platform is right for you, consider your goals. If you want to showcase a diverse range of skills and create a comprehensive online presence, a personal website might be a better fit. If your primary goal is to showcase visual work, a portfolio is a more streamlined option.

Essential Elements of a Powerful Online Presence

Regardless of the platform you choose, certain elements are essential for creating a compelling online presence:

1. **About Me:** Introduce yourself, your background, and your career goals. Share your story in an authentic and engagingway.

2. **Skills and Experience:** Highlight your most relevant skills, experiences, and accomplishments. Use keywords that align with your target job roles.

3. **Work Samples:** Showcase your best work. This could include writing samples, design projects, code repositories, or any other relevant examples of your skills and expertise.

4. **Testimonials:** If you have any positive feedback from clients, colleagues, or mentors, include it on your website or portfolio. Testimonials add credibility and social proof.

5. **Contact Information:** Make it easy for potential employers to get in touch with you. Include your email address, LinkedIn profile, and any other relevant contact

information.

6.   **Call to Action:** Guide visitors on what you want them to do next. Do you want them to contact you for a job? View your portfolio? Subscribe to your blog? Make your intentions clear.

Tips for Creating a Standout Digital Showcase

- **Keep it Simple:** Don't overcomplicate your design. A clean, uncluttered layout is easier to navigate and more visually appealing.

- **Use High-Quality Visuals:** If you're showcasing visual work, make sure your images and videos are high quality and optimized for the web.

- **Tell a Story:** Use your website or portfolio to tell a compelling story about your career journey. Highlight your challenges, successes, and lessons learned.

- **Proofread Carefully:** Typos and grammatical errors can damage your credibility. Proofread your content carefully before publishing.

- **Update Regularly:** Keep your website or portfolio up-to-date with your latest work and achievements. This shows potential employers that you're active and engaged in your field.

Resources for Building Your Online Presence

- **Website Builders:** If you're not tech-savvy,

website builders like Wix, Squarespace, or WordPress offer user-friendly drag-and-drop interfaces for creating professional-looking websites.

• **Portfolio Platforms:** For showcasing visual work, platforms like Behance, Dribbble, and Carbonmade offer easy-to-use templates and features.

• **LinkedIn:** Don't underestimate the power of LinkedIn. Optimize your profile, join relevant groups, and share your work and insights to build your professional network.

Your Online Presence: A Continuous Work in Progress

Remember, your online presence isn't a one-and-done project. It's a continuous work in progress that evolves as you grow and develop in your career. As you gain new skills, experiences, and accomplishments, update your website or portfolio to reflect yourprogress.

By investing in your online presence, you're not just creating a digital resume; you're building a powerful tool for attracting opportunities and taking your career to the next level.

Chapter 11: The Power of Follow-Up

You've crafted a stellar resume, nailed the interview, and left a lasting impression. So, now what? Do you simply wait by thephone, hoping for a call?

Absolutely not.

In the "Hire Your Boss" playbook, the job search doesn't end after the interview. In fact, it's far from over. This is where the power offollow-up comes into play.

Think of it like this: you've made a great first impression, but you need to keep the momentum going. Following up shows your genuine interest, keeps you top-of-mind, and demonstrates your initiative – qualities that any boss would value.

But follow-up isn't just about sending a generic thank-you email. It's a strategic process that can make or break your chances of landing the job.

In this chapter, we'll explore:

• Why follow-up is crucial in the "Hire Your Boss" framework.

• The different types of follow-up and when to use them.

• How to craft compelling follow-up messages that getnoticed.

• The art of timing and persistence in follow-up.

• Common mistakes to avoid in your follow-up

efforts.

The Stakes Are High

Don't underestimate the impact of a well-executed follow-up. It can:

• **Set you apart from the competition:** Most applicants don't follow up effectively, so doing so can give you a significant edge.

• **Reinforce your value proposition:** Remind the hiring manager why you're the ideal candidate for the job.

• **Address any lingering questions:** Clarify any doubts or concerns the interviewer might have.

• **Build rapport and create a positive impression:** Show your professionalism and enthusiasm for the opportunity.

By mastering the art of follow-up, you're not just checking a box; you're demonstrating your commitment, proactivity, and genuine interest in the role. These are qualities that any boss would be thrilled to have in their team.

Ready to Take Action?

Get ready to elevate your job search game with the power of follow-up. We'll delve into practical tips, real-world examples, and actionable strategies that you can implement immediately.

By the end of this chapter, you'll be equipped with the knowledge and confidence to follow up effectively and secure your dreamjob.

So, let's dive in and discover how to leave a lasting impression thatgets you hired.

Staying Top-of-Mind

Landing an interview is a significant achievement, but it's just one step in the "Hire Your Boss" journey. To truly make an impact, you need to stay top-of-mind with potential employers. This doesn't mean bombarding them with emails or calls, but rather strategically positioning yourself as a proactive and engaged candidate.

The Power of a Timely Follow-Up

A well-crafted follow-up can serve multiple purposes:

1.   **Expressing Gratitude:** It shows your appreciation for the opportunity to interview or be considered for the position.

2.   **Reiterating Interest:** It reaffirms your enthusiasm for the role and the company.

3.   **Providing Additional Information:** It gives you a chance to share any relevant details you might have missed during the interview.

4.   **Staying Connected:** It keeps the conversation going and positions you as a proactive communicator.

Crafting the Perfect Follow-Up Email

While a handwritten thank-you note can be a nice touch,

email is the most common and efficient way to follow up in today's job market. Here's a basic outline for a follow-up email:

- **Subject Line:** Keep it concise and specific, e.g., "Thank You

  - [Your Name] - [Job Title] Interview."

- **Salutation:** Address the hiring manager or recruiter by name if possible.

- **First Paragraph:** Express your gratitude for the interview opportunity and reiterate your interest in the position.

- **Second Paragraph:** Briefly summarize your qualifications and highlight how your skills align with the company's needs. You can also mention a specific topic discussed during the interview to personalize the message.

- **Third Paragraph:** Express your eagerness to hear back and offer to provide any additional information if needed.

- **Closing:** Thank them again for their time and consideration. Include your contact information.

Sample Follow-Up Email

Subject: Thank You - [Your Name] - Marketing Manager InterviewDear [Hiring Manager Name],

Thank you for taking the time to interview me for the Marketing Manager position at [Company Name]. I thoroughly enjoyed our conversation and was impressed by your team's innovative approach to [mention a specific project or initiative].

As we discussed, my [number] years of experience in [mention your relevant experience] have equipped me with the skills and expertise necessary to [mention how you can contribute to the company's goals]. I am particularly excited about the opportunity to [mention a specific aspect of the job that interests you].

I am eager to hear about the next steps in the hiring process. Please don't hesitate to contact me if you require any further information or references.

Thank you again for your time and consideration.Sincerely,

[Your Name]

Timing Your Follow-Up

Timing is crucial when it comes to follow-up. Here's a general guideline:

• **After an Application:** If you haven't heard back within a week or two, send a brief email to confirm receipt of your application and reiterate your interest in the position.

• **After an Interview:** Send a thank-you email within 24 hours of the interview. If you haven't heard back within thetimeframe discussed during the interview, follow up with a polite email to inquire about the status of your application.

The Art of the Follow-Up Phone Call

In some cases, a follow-up phone call may be

appropriate, especially if you have a strong rapport with the interviewer or if email communication has been unsuccessful. Keep the call brief and professional, and reiterate your interest in the position.

When to Move On

If you haven't heard back after multiple follow-ups, it's okay to move on. Don't take it personally; hiring processes can be lengthy and unpredictable. Focus your energy on other opportunities and continue to hone your "Hire Your Boss" skills.

Beyond the Job Search

Remember, the "Hire Your Boss" mindset isn't just for job seekers. It's a valuable tool for career development and relationship building. Stay in touch with your network, offer support and advice, and continue to cultivate meaningful connections.

In Summary

By implementing a strategic follow-up plan, you can increase your chances of landing your dream job. Remember, staying top-of-mind is about more than just sending emails; it's about demonstrating your professionalism, enthusiasm, and commitment to the role.

By following these guidelines and tailoring your follow-ups to each specific situation, you'll leave a lasting impression and position yourself as a top candidate for any role.

Thank You Notes and Emails

Imagine this: You've just aced an interview. You answered every question with confidence, your personality shined through, and you felt a genuine connection with the hiring manager. You're on cloud nine, convinced this could be *the* job. But then, radio silence. Days turn into weeks, and you start to wonder if you misread the situation. Did you say something wrong? Did they findsomeone else?

Before you spiral into self-doubt, let me introduce you to a secret weapon that can make all the difference: the humble thank you note or email.

Why Thank You Notes Matter

In a world of impersonal communication and digital overload, a heartfelt thank you note or email can be a breath of fresh air. It's a simple gesture that shows you're not just another applicant; you're a thoughtful, appreciative professional who values their time.

But it's not just about good manners. Thank you notes have a real impact on your job prospects. Studies have shown that candidates who send thank you notes are more likely to be remembered by hiring managers and are perceived as more professional and engaged. (Smith, 2018).

The Power of Gratitude and Reiteration

Your thank you note isn't just a formality; it's an opportunity to:

1. **Express Gratitude:** Sincerely thank the interviewer for their time and consideration. This shows respect and leaves a positive impression.

2. **Reiterate Your Interest:** Remind the interviewer why you're excited about the role and how your skills and experience align with their needs. This reinforces your enthusiasm and qualifications.

3. **Address Any Concerns:** If there were any questions you didn't answer fully during the interview, use the thank you note to provide additional information or clarify your points.

4. **Ask a Question:** If appropriate, ask a thoughtful question related to the position or the company. This shows you're engaged and eager to learn more.

5. **Stay Top-of-Mind:** By sending a thank you note, you keep your name fresh in the interviewer's mind as they make their decision.

When and How to Send Your Thank You

Timing is key when it comes to thank you notes. Aim to send your note within 24-48 hours of the interview. This ensures your message is still relevant and fresh in the interviewer's mind.

As for the format, both handwritten notes and emails are acceptable. Handwritten notes can add a personal touch, while emails are often more convenient and timely.

Ultimately, the choice is yours.

Crafting Your Thank You Note: A Step-by-Step Guide

Here's a simple structure you can follow:

1. **Subject Line (Email):**

- Keep it concise and relevant.

- Examples: "Thank you for the interview – [Your Name]" or "Follow up regarding [Job Title] position."

2. **Salutation:**

- Address the interviewer by name (e.g., "Dear Ms. Smith").

- If you interviewed with multiple people, send individual notes to each person.

3. **Opening Paragraph:**

- Express your gratitude for the interview opportunity.

- Mention something specific you discussed during the interview that resonated with you.

4. **Middle Paragraph(s):**

- Reiterate your interest in the position and why you're a good fit.

- Highlight specific skills or experiences that align with the job requirements.

- Address any concerns or questions the interviewer

may have had.

5. Closing Paragraph:

- Thank the interviewer again for their time and consideration.

- Express your enthusiasm for the next steps in the hiring process.

- Offer to provide any additional information they may need.

6. Signature:

- Sign off professionally (e.g., "Sincerely," "Best regards," or "Thank you").

- Include your full name, phone number, and email address.

Sample Thank You Email:

Subject: Thank you for the interview – [Your Name] Dear [Interviewer Name],

Thank you for taking the time to interview me for the [Job Title] position yesterday. I enjoyed learning more about the role and your company's mission. I was particularly impressed by your commitment to [mention something specific discussed during the interview].

As we discussed, my [highlight a specific skill or experience] would be a valuable asset to your team. I'm confident that my passion for [mention a relevant interest or skill] and my experience in [mention relevant experience] make me an ideal candidate for thisposition.

Thank you again for your time and consideration. I'm excited about the opportunity to join your team and contribute to your company's success. Please feel free to contact me if you have any further questions.

Sincerely, [Your Name]

Common Mistakes to Avoid:

• **Generic Messages:** Personalize your note and avoidgeneric phrases.

• **Typos or Grammatical Errors:** Proofread your notecarefully before sending it.

• **Overly Lengthy Notes:** Keep your message concise andfocused.

• **Sending Too Late:** Aim to send your note within 24-48hours of the interview.

• **Being Overly Casual:** Maintain a professional tonethroughout your note.

The Bottom Line

A well-crafted thank you note or email is a simple yet powerful tool that can set you apart from other candidates and leave a lasting positive impression. By expressing your gratitude, reiterating your interest, and addressing any concerns, you'll demonstrate your professionalism, enthusiasm, and commitment to the role.

So, the next time you leave an interview feeling confident,

don't let that momentum fade away. Take a few minutes to send a heartfelt thank you note or email, and watch it work its magic. It could be the final touch that lands you your dream job.

Maintaining Relationships:

Networking isn't a one-and-done activity. Think of it like gardening: planting the seeds (initial connections) is just the first step. To reap the rewards (job opportunities, career advancement), you need to consistently nurture those relationships.

In this section, we'll explore how to keep your network engaged, build trust, and ensure that you're top of mind when opportunities arise. Remember, it's about more than just asking for favors; it's about cultivating genuine connections that benefit both you and your contacts.

The Art of Staying Connected

Staying connected doesn't mean bombarding your network with daily emails or LinkedIn messages. It's about finding the right balance of communication that feels natural and authentic. Hereare some strategies:

- **Regular Check-Ins:** Reach out to your contacts periodically to see how they're doing. Ask about their projects, challenges, or simply how their day is going. Show genuineinterest in their lives.

- **Share Relevant Information:** When you come

across articles, resources, or job postings that might be of interest to your contacts, pass them along. This demonstrates that you're thinking of them and adds value to their professional lives.

• **Celebrate Their Wins:** Congratulate your contacts on their accomplishments, promotions, or new endeavors. A simple message or comment can go a long way in strengthening your connection.

• **Offer Help:** If you see an opportunity to help your contacts, don't hesitate. Offer to introduce them to someone in your network, share your expertise, or simply lend a listening ear.

Building Trust and Reciprocity

Networking is a two-way street. To build strong, lasting relationships, you need to give as much as you receive.

• **Be a Resource:** Offer your knowledge, skills, and connections to help your contacts achieve their goals. Become a valuable asset in their network.

• **Follow Through:** When you make a commitment, deliver on it. If you promise to introduce someone or share a resource, do it promptly and professionally.

• **Show Appreciation:** Always express gratitude for the help and support you receive from your network. A simple thank-you note or email can go a long way.

Leveraging Technology for Connection

Technology can be a powerful tool for maintaining relationships,but it's important to use it strategically.

- **LinkedIn:** Stay active on LinkedIn by sharing updates, commenting on posts, and joining groups relevant to your industry. Connect with new people and strengthen existingrelationships.

- **Email Newsletters:** Consider creating a newsletter to shareupdates on your career, industry insights, or valuable resources. This keeps you on the radar of your network.

- **Virtual Coffee Chats:** Schedule virtual coffee chats or catch-up calls with your contacts to maintain face-to-face interaction.

Maintaining Relationships with Different Types of Contacts

Remember, your network is diverse, and each relationshiprequires a different approach.

- **Mentors:** Express your gratitude for their guidance and support. Keep them updated on your progress and seek their advice when needed.

- **Colleagues:** Stay in touch even after you change jobs. Offer support and collaborate on projects whenever possible.

- **Industry Leaders:** Engage with their content, comment on their posts, and attend their speaking events.

- **Potential Employers:** Stay on their radar by

following their company pages, engaging with their content, and reaching out periodically to express your interest.

The Long Game

Building and maintaining a strong network takes time and effort. Don't expect instant results. Focus on building genuine connections and providing value, and the rewards will come.

As Porter Gale states in *Your Network is Your Net Worth*, "Your network is your net worth." (Gale 2013, 11) Investing in your network is an investment in your career. By nurturing relationships, you're creating a powerful support system that can open doors, provide opportunities, and help you achieve your professional goals.

Remember, the "Hire Your Boss" framework is not just about landing a job; it's about building a fulfilling career. By maintaining strong relationships with your network, you're setting yourself up for long-term success.

Chapter 12: Handling Rejection and Setbacks

Let's face it: rejection stings. Whether it's an unanswered job application, a disappointing interview outcome, or even a flat-out "no," setbacks are an inevitable part of the job search journey. But here's the secret: rejection isn't the end; it's merely a redirection. It's a chance to pause, reassess, and ultimately, refine your approach.

In this chapter, we'll delve into the art of handling rejection with resilience and grace. We'll explore how to reframe setbacks as opportunities for growth, how to extract valuable feedback from negative experiences, and how to bounce back stronger and moredetermined than ever.

Rejection: Your Unexpected Ally

While it may seem counterintuitive, rejection can actually be a valuable ally in your quest to hire your boss. It can reveal blind spots in your clarity, highlight areas where your positioning could be stronger, and help you fine-tune your alignment with potential employers.

Think of rejection as a course correction, nudging you back on track toward a more fulfilling and aligned career path. It's a chance to ask yourself some tough but essential questions:

• Did I truly understand the job requirements and companyculture?

- Did my application and interview effectively showcase my unique value proposition?

- Was this company truly the right fit for my career goalsand values?

By analyzing your setbacks through the lens of clarity, positioning,and alignment, you can transform rejection into a powerful tool for self-discovery and improvement.

Embrace the Feedback Loop

Every rejection is a learning opportunity, but only if you're willing to embrace the feedback loop. Rather than dwelling on disappointment, take a proactive approach:

- **Request Feedback:** Reach out to the hiring manager or recruiter and politely ask for specific feedback on yourapplication or interview. Their insights can be invaluable inidentifying areas for growth.

- **Analyze the Feedback:** Reflect on the feedback you receive and look for patterns or recurring themes. Are there certain skills you need to strengthen? Is your communication style not resonating with employers? Use this information to refine your approach.

- **Adjust Your Strategy:** Based on your analysis, make necessary adjustments to your resume, cover letters, interviewing style, or even your target companies.

By actively seeking feedback and using it to refine your job search strategy, you'll increase your chances of landing the rightopportunity.

Bouncing Back with Resilience

Resilience is the ability to bounce back from setbacks, learn from them, and keep moving forward. It's a critical skill for anyone navigating the ups and downs of the job search.

Here are some tips for cultivating resilience:

• **Acknowledge Your Emotions:** It's okay to feel disappointed or discouraged. Allow yourself to process these emotions, but don't let them consume you.

• **Maintain a Positive Outlook:** Focus on your strengths and accomplishments. Remember that one rejection doesn't define your worth or your potential.

• **Surround Yourself with Support:** Lean on your network of family, friends, mentors, or career coaches for encouragement and advice.

• **Celebrate Small Wins:** Acknowledge your progress, even if it's just landing an interview or receiving positive feedback. These small victories can fuel your motivation and keep you going.

• **Focus on the Long Game:** Remember that the job search is a marathon, not a sprint. Stay committed to your goals and keep refining your approach until you find the right fit.

In this chapter, we'll dive deeper into the art of handling rejection and setbacks, providing you with practical strategies, inspiring stories, and actionable advice to turn those "no's" into your next "yes."

Resilience and Growth

Rejection is a natural part of the job search process. It's inevitable, and it can be incredibly disheartening. However, with the right mindset, you can transform rejection from a painful setback into a powerful catalyst for growth and improvement.

Why Rejection Hurts (and Why It Shouldn't)

Our brains are wired to perceive rejection as a threat to our social standing and self-worth. When we're rejected, our bodies release stress hormones like cortisol, which can trigger feelings of anxiety, sadness, and even anger.[1]

But here's the thing: rejection in the job search rarely reflects your inherent worth or abilities. It's often a matter of fit, timing, or simply not being the right match for a particular role or company. Understanding this can help you detach your emotions from the outcome and view rejection with a more objective lens.

The Growth Mindset: Your Secret Weapon

One of the most powerful tools you can cultivate in the face of rejection is a growth mindset. Coined by psychologist Carol Dweck, a growth mindset is the belief that your abilities and intelligence can be developed through dedication and hard work.

People with a growth mindset view challenges as opportunities to learn and grow. They embrace feedback, seek out new experiences, and persist in the face of setbacks. This mindset is essential for navigating the ups and downs of the job search.

Turning Rejection into a Stepping Stone

So, how do you actually reframe rejection as an opportunity for growth? Here are some practical strategies:

1. **Analyze and Learn:** Don't just brush off rejection. Take time to reflect on what you can learn from it. Was there something in your resume or cover letter that could be improved? Did you miss a key point in the interview? Could you have done more research on the company? Use rejection as a feedback loop to refine your approach.

2. **Seek Feedback:** If possible, ask for feedback from the interviewer or hiring manager. While not everyone will be willing to provide it, those who do can offer valuable insights into your strengths and weaknesses.

3. **Adjust Your Strategy:** Based on your analysis and feedback, make adjustments to your job search strategy. This could involve updating your resume, practicing your interviewing skills, or targeting different types ofcompanies.

4. **Don't Take It Personally:** Remember, rejection is rarely a personal attack. It's often a matter of circumstances beyond your control. Don't let rejection damage your self-

confidence or deter you from pursuing your goals.

5.   **Celebrate Small Wins:** The job search is a marathon, not a sprint. Celebrate every small victory, whether it's landing an interview, receiving positive feedback, or expanding your network. These wins will keep you motivated and focused on your long-term goals.

The Resilience Factor

Resilience is the ability to bounce back from setbacks and keep moving forward. It's a crucial trait for navigating the job search and achieving your career goals.

Building resilience takes time and practice. Here are a few tips:

•   **Cultivate a Positive Attitude:** Focus on your strengths, celebrate your achievements, and maintain a hopeful outlook.

•   **Build a Strong Support Network:** Surround yourself with supportive friends, family, and mentors who can offer encouragement and guidance.

•   **Take Care of Yourself:** Prioritize your physical and mental health. Exercise, eat well, get enough sleep, and practice stress-reducing activities.

•   **Set Realistic Expectations:** Don't expect to land your dream job overnight. Set achievable goals and focus on progress, not perfection.

•   **Learn from Role Models:** Read stories of

successful peoplewho have overcome rejection and adversity. Their resilience can inspire you to keep going.

Remember: Rejection is Not the End

Rejection is not a reflection of your worth or potential. It's simply a hurdle on your path to success. By embracing a growth mindset, learning from your experiences, and cultivating resilience, you can turn rejection into a stepping stone towards landing your dream job.

Seeking Feedback

No one likes rejection. It stings, it deflates, and it can make you question your entire career path. But what if I told you that rejection could be one of your most valuable tools in the "Hire Your Boss" process? It's true. Feedback, even when it comes in the form of a "no," is a goldmine of insights that can help you refine your approach, improve your skills, and ultimately land that dreamjob.

Why Feedback is Essential

Think of feedback as a personal trainer for your job search. Just asa trainer observes your form and technique to help you improve your workouts, feedback from potential employers provides you with valuable insights into how you're perceived in the job market.

This isn't about dwelling on your shortcomings or beating yourselfup. It's about gaining a clearer understanding of your strengths and weaknesses, so you can make strategic adjustments to your Clarity, Positioning, and Alignment.

Types of Feedback

Feedback can come in many forms:

• **Direct Feedback:** This is the most straightforward kind of feedback. It might come in the form of a rejection email that explains why you weren't selected, or it could be verbal feedback from an interviewer.

• **Indirect Feedback:** This is feedback that you glean from the interview process itself. Did the interviewer seem engaged and interested? Did they ask follow-up questions? Did they offer any hints about what they were looking for in a candidate?

• **Self-Reflection:** This is the feedback you give yourself. Take some time after each interview to reflect on what went well and what could be improved. Were you nervous? Did you communicate your value proposition effectively? Did you ask insightful questions?

How to Ask for Feedback

While some employers may offer feedback voluntarily, don't beafraid to ask for it. Here are some tips:

• **Be gracious:** Thank the interviewer for their time and consideration.

• **Be specific:** Don't just ask for "feedback." Ask for specific insights on how you could improve your interview skills or better tailor your resume to the position.

- **Be professional:** Avoid getting defensive or argumentative. Remember, you're seeking feedback to learn and grow, notto prove anyone wrong.

What to Do with Feedback

Once you've received feedback, it's time to put it to work:

- **Analyze and Reflect:** Carefully review the feedback you've received. Look for patterns and common themes.

- **Identify Areas for Improvement:** Are there specific skills you need to develop? Is your resume not highlighting your most relevant experiences? Do you need to refine your interview approach?

- **Take Action:** Develop a plan to address the areas where you need to improve. This might involve taking courses, attending workshops, or seeking out a mentor.

Case Study: Turning Rejection into a Job Offer

Sarah, a marketing professional, was repeatedly rejected for positions she felt well-qualified for. Frustrated, she started asking for feedback after each interview. One hiring manager told her that while her resume was impressive, she didn't seem passionate about the company's mission during the interview.

This feedback was a wake-up call for Sarah. She realized that she had been focusing too much on her skills and experience and not enough on her enthusiasm for the specific companies she was applying to. She took the time to research each company thoroughly, tailor her cover letters to their specific needs, and practice expressing her genuine interest in their work.

The result? Sarah landed her dream job at a company whose mission truly resonated with her. She credits her success to the feedback she received, which helped her refine her Clarity, Positioning, and Alignment.

Embracing a Growth Mindset

The "Hire Your Boss" mindset is all about taking ownership of your career and embracing a growth mindset. Feedback, whether positive or negative, is a gift. It's an opportunity to learn, improve, and ultimately achieve your goals.

Remember, the job search is a journey, not a destination. There will be bumps along the road, but with the right tools and mindset, you can navigate any challenge. By actively seeking feedback and using it to your advantage, you'll become a more confident, capable, and successful job seeker.

As you continue your "Hire Your Boss" journey, remember that feedback is your ally. Don't shy away from it; embrace it. Let it guide you towards the career you deserve.

Overcoming Discouragement

The job search isn't always a smooth ride. There will be

bumps, detours, and even the occasional roadblock. Rejection, unanswered applications, and seemingly endless waiting can drain your energy and dampen your spirits. But here's the thing: every successful job seeker has faced these challenges. The difference lies in how they respond.

The Discouragement Dip: It's Normal (and Temporary)

Feeling discouraged during your job search is completely normal. It's important to acknowledge these feelings, rather than suppress them. Trying to force positivity when you're feeling down can be counterproductive. Allow yourself to feel the frustration, but don'tlet it consume you.

Instead, reframe discouragement as a temporary dip, a natural part of the process. Remember, the job search is a marathon, not a sprint. There will be ups and downs along the way. The key is to develop resilience and keep moving forward.

Strategies for Staying Motivated

Here are some practical strategies to help you maintain motivationand persevere through challenging times:

1. **Set Realistic Expectations:** Don't expect to find your dream job overnight. The job search takes time, effort, and patience. Set realistic goals for yourself, such as applying to a certain number of jobs each week or attending networking events regularly. Celebrate small wins along the

way to keep your spirits high.

2.   **Practice Self-Care:** Don't neglect your physical and mental well-being during your job search. Get enough sleep, eat healthy foods, exercise regularly, and take time for activities you enjoy. Taking care of yourself will give you the energy and resilience you need to keep going.

3.   **Build a Support Network:** Surround yourself with positive and supportive people. Share your challenges and successes with friends, family, mentors, or a career coach. They can offer encouragement, advice, and a listening ear when you need it most.

4.   **Revisit Your "Why":** Remind yourself why you're on this journey. What are your career goals? What are you passionate about? What impact do you want to make? Reconnecting with your purpose can reignite your motivation and give you a renewed sense of direction.

5.   **Learn from Setbacks:** Don't view rejection as a failure, but as a learning opportunity. If you receive a rejection, try to get feedback from the employer. This can help you identify areas for improvement and refine your approach.

6.   **Celebrate Your Strengths:** Don't dwell on your weaknesses. Instead, focus on your strengths and accomplishments. Make a list of your skills, experiences, and achievements. This can boost your confidence and remind you of your value.

7.   **Take a Break:** If you're feeling overwhelmed, take a break from the job search for a day or two. Go for a walk, watch a movie, or spend time with loved ones. A change of pace can help you recharge and return to your search with renewed energy.

8.   **Seek Professional Help:** If you're struggling to cope with discouragement, consider seeking professional help. A therapist or career counselor can provide support, guidance, and tools to help you manage stress and stay motivated.

The Power of Perseverance

Remember, the job search is a journey, not a destination. It's about perseverance, resilience, and unwavering belief in yourself. By staying focused on your goals, taking care of yourself, and learning from your experiences, you can overcome any obstacles and land the job of your dreams.

As Winston Churchill famously said, "Success is not final, failure is not fatal: it is the courage to continue that counts." Keep going. Your perseverance will pay off.

Chapter 13: Staying Ahead: Continuous Learning and Growth

Congratulations! You've landed your dream job, hired the perfect boss, and are well on your way to a fulfilling career. But hold on – the journey doesn't end here. In fact, it's just the beginning.

Consider this: The skills and knowledge that got you to this point might not be enough to keep you thriving in the long run. The world is constantly evolving, and so are the demands of the job market. To stay ahead of the curve, you need to embrace continuous learning and growth as a core part of your career strategy.

Think of it this way: Your career isn't a sprint; it's a marathon. You wouldn't expect to run a marathon without proper training, would you? The same principle applies to your professional life. To stay competitive, motivated, and adaptable, you need to invest in yourself.

Why Continuous Learning Matters

In today's fast-paced world, skills can become obsolete quickly. New technologies emerge, industries shift, and job roles evolve. If you're not actively learning and expanding your skillset, you risk becoming stagnant and falling behind.

But continuous learning isn't just about staying relevant – it'sabout personal and professional growth. It's about pushing yourself beyond your comfort zone, exploring new ideas, and discovering hidden talents. It's about becoming the best version ofyourself.

The Benefits of Investing in Yourself

Investing in your own learning and development offers a wealth ofbenefits:

- **Increased Earning Potential:** Individuals who continually upgrade their skills are more likely to command higher salaries and secure promotions.

- **Enhanced Job Satisfaction:** Learning new things keeps your work engaging and challenging, preventing burnout and boredom.

- **Improved Adaptability:** A broad skillset allows you to pivotwith ease in a changing job market, opening up new opportunities.

- **Boosted Confidence:** Mastering new skills builds your confidence and empowers you to take on bigger challenges.

In this chapter, we'll explore practical strategies for incorporating continuous learning into your career plan. We'll discuss how to identify the most relevant skills to develop, where to find resources for learning, and how to make learning a sustainable habit.

Whether you're a seasoned professional or just starting out, this chapter will provide you with the tools and inspiration to embrace lifelong learning and take your career to new heights.

Investing in Yourself

In today's rapidly evolving professional landscape, the phrase "what got you here won't get you there" rings truer than ever. The skills and knowledge that landed you your current job may not be sufficient to propel you to the next level or even keep you relevant in a few years. That's why ongoing professional development is not just a nice-to-have, but a non-negotiable for anyone serious about "hiring their boss" and taking charge of their career trajectory.

Think of your career as a marathon, not a sprint. Just as athletes need to train consistently to stay in peak condition, professionals must continually invest in their skills and knowledge to remain competitive and adaptable. In fact, research has shown a direct correlation between lifelong learning and career success. A study by the University of Phoenix found that 87% of adults who engage in ongoing learning report feeling more confident in their job performance.

Why Investing in Yourself Matters

Investing in your professional development isn't just about adding another line to your resume or acquiring a new certification (though those are certainly valuable). It's about cultivating a growth mindset, expanding your skillset, and increasing your valueproposition.

Here are some key benefits of continuous learning:

• **Enhancing Your Skillset:** Learning new skills or deepening existing ones can make you a more versatile and valuable employee. This can open doors to new opportunities and increase your earning potential.

• **Boosting Your Confidence:** As you gain knowledge and expertise, you'll naturally feel more confident in your abilities. This confidence can translate into better job performance, stronger networking skills, and more successful interviews.

• **Staying Relevant:** Industries are constantly evolving, with new technologies and trends emerging at a rapid pace. Continuous learning helps you stay ahead of the curve and avoid becoming obsolete.

• **Expanding Your Network:** Learning often involves interacting with other professionals, attending conferences, or joining online communities. These activities can expand your network and open doors to new connections and opportunities.

• **Increasing Your Job Satisfaction:** Learning new things can be intrinsically motivating and lead to increased job satisfaction. When you're constantly growing and developing, your work feels less like a chore and more like a fulfilling pursuit.

How to Invest in Yourself

Investing in yourself doesn't have to be expensive or time-consuming. There are countless resources available to help you learn and grow, both online and offline. Here are a few ideas:

•	**Take Online Courses:** Platforms like Coursera, Udemy, LinkedIn Learning, and edX offer a vast array of courses on virtually any topic you can imagine. Many of these courses are free or very affordable.

•	**Read Books and Articles:** Stay up-to-date on industry trends and thought leadership by reading books, articles, and blogs from experts in your field.

•	**Attend Conferences and Workshops:** These events offer a great opportunity to learn from experts, network with other professionals, and stay abreast of the latest developments in your industry.

•	**Find a Mentor:** A mentor can provide valuable guidance, support, and insights as you navigate your career journey.

•	**Join Professional Organizations:** These organizations often offer training programs, networking events, and other resources to help their members grow professionally.

•	**Volunteer:** Volunteering your time and skills can help you develop new skills, gain experience, and make a differencein your community.

- **Take on New Challenges at Work:** Look for opportunities to stretch yourself and take on new responsibilities at your current job. This can help you learn new skills anddemonstrate your initiative to your employer.

Make Learning a Habit

The most successful professionals make learning a habit, not just a one-time event. They set aside time each week to read, listen to podcasts, take online courses, or attend industry events. They see learning as an investment in themselves, and they reap the rewards in the form of career advancement, increased earning potential, and greater job satisfaction.

Your Learning Journey

Remember, your learning journey is unique to you. What works for one person may not work for another. Experiment with different learning methods and find what resonates with you. The most important thing is to be consistent and make learning a priority.

By investing in yourself, you're not just preparing for the next job; you're preparing for a fulfilling and successful career. You're taking charge of your professional destiny and positioning yourself for long-term growth and success.

Skill Enhancement

You've got the "Hire Your Boss" mindset, a clear career vision, and a killer personal brand. But let's face it, even the most seasoned professionals have room for growth. In this section, we'll delve into how to identify your skill gaps, bridge them with targeted training and certifications, and ultimately, increase your value in the job market.

Why Skill Enhancement Matters

The professional landscape is constantly evolving. New technologies emerge, industries shift, and in-demand skills change. To stay ahead of the curve and remain competitive, you need to commit to continuous learning and development.

Investing in yourself through skill enhancement isn't just about checking boxes on your resume; it's about expanding your capabilities, boosting your confidence, and demonstrating your commitment to growth. This can make you a more attractive candidate to potential employers and set you up for long-term career success.

Uncovering Your Skill Gaps: A Three-Step Approach

1. **Self-Assessment:** Start by honestly evaluating your strengths and weaknesses. What skills are you confident in? Where do you feel you could improve? Consider using online self-assessment tools or seeking feedback from colleagues and mentors.

2. **Market Research:** Research the skills that are in high demand for your target roles. Job postings, industry reports, and online resources like LinkedIn can provide

valuable insights.

3.   **Gap Analysis:** Compare your self-assessment and market research findings. Identify the areas where your skills don't quite match up with what employers are seeking. These are your skill gaps.

Bridging the Gap: Training and Certifications

Once you've identified your skill gaps, it's time to take action. Luckily, there are a plethora of options available for skill development:

• **Online Courses and Tutorials:** Platforms like Coursera, Udemy, and LinkedIn Learning offer a vast array of courses on everything from coding to project management to public speaking.

• **Workshops and Seminars:** Attend in-person or virtual workshops and seminars to learn from experts in your field and network with other professionals.

• **Certifications:** Earning industry-recognized certifications can demonstrate your expertise and commitment to your field.

• **Mentorship and Coaching:** Seek out mentors who can offer guidance and support as you develop new skills. Consider investing in a career coach to help you navigate your career path.

• **On-the-Job Learning:** Take on new challenges at

work, volunteer for projects, or shadow colleagues in different roles to gain hands-on experience.

Remember, the best learning path for you will depend on your specific needs and preferences. Don't be afraid to experiment and try different approaches until you find what works best for you.

Choosing the Right Training and Certifications

Not all training and certifications are created equal. When selecting programs, consider the following factors:

• **Relevance:** Choose programs that align with your career goals and the skills in demand in your industry.

• **Quality:** Research the reputation of the provider, read reviews from past participants, and ensure the program is up-to-date and comprehensive.

• **Cost:** Consider your budget and weigh the potential return on investment. Some training programs may be expensive,but if they lead to a significant career advancement, they may be worth the investment.

• **Format:** Choose a format that fits your learning style and schedule. Some people prefer self-paced online courses, while others thrive in interactive workshops.

Showcasing Your New Skills

Once you've acquired new skills or certifications, don't be shy about showcasing them. Update your resume, LinkedIn profile, and online portfolio to reflect your newfound expertise. Mention your accomplishments during networking conversations and job interviews.

By proactively addressing your skill gaps, you're not just making yourself a more attractive candidate; you're investing in your own professional growth and future success. As the saying goes, "The only person you are destined to become is the person you decide to be" (Ralph Waldo Emerson, *Self-Reliance*, 1841). By committing to continuous learning, you're taking ownership of your career destiny and paving the way for a brighter future.

Resources for Skill Enhancement

Here are a few resources to get you started on your skill-enhancement journey:

• **Coursera:** Offers a wide range of online courses from topuniversities and institutions (Coursera, n.d.).

• **Udemy:** Provides thousands of affordable online courseson various topics (Udemy, n.d.).

• **LinkedIn Learning:** Offers video-based courses on business, technology, and creative skills (LinkedIn Learning, n.d.).

• **edX:** Provides free online courses from top universities(edX, n.d.).

Remember, the best resource for you is the one that best suits your individual needs and learning style. Explore your options and find the training that will help you reach your full potential.

In the Next Section...

In the next section, we'll shift our focus to the importance of adapting to change and staying ahead of the curve in the ever-evolving professional landscape.

Adapting to Change

The professional landscape is far from static. Industries evolve, technologies emerge, and the skills in demand today might be obsolete tomorrow. Embracing change isn't just about survival; it's about thriving. To "Hire Your Boss" effectively, you must become a lifelong learner, continually adapting to the ever-shifting currents of your field.

Think of yourself as a surfer. You wouldn't paddle out with a board meant for calm waters if you're facing a tsunami, right? Similarly, the skills and knowledge you acquired yesterday might not be enough to ride the wave of tomorrow's opportunities.

The Perils of Stagnation

Failing to stay current can have dire consequences for your career. You risk becoming irrelevant, missing out on opportunities, and ultimately, finding yourself "unhirable." A study by the World Economic Forum predicts that by 2025, over half of all employees will need significant reskilling and upskilling to remain competitive.

The Power of Continuous Learning

The good news is that you have the power to shape your professional destiny through continuous learning. By actively seeking new knowledge and skills, you not only enhance your value proposition but also signal to potential employers that you're adaptable, curious, and committed to growth.

Here are some practical strategies to stay ahead of the curve:

1. **Become a News Junkie (for Your Industry):** Subscribe to industry publications, follow relevant blogs and social media accounts, and set up Google Alerts for keywords related to your field. Dedicate time each week to reading articles, listening to podcasts, or watching webinars.

2. **Network with Purpose:** Attend industry conferences, join professional associations, and engage in online forums. Connect with thought leaders, ask questions, and share your insights. Networking is not just about who you know; it's about what you learn from those connections. (Smith, 2020)

3. **Embrace Lifelong Learning:** Enroll in online courses, attend workshops, or pursue advanced certifications. Many platforms offer free or affordable resources for professional development. Don't be afraid to step outside your comfort zone and explore new areas of knowledge.

4. **Experiment and Tinker:** If you're in a tech-related field, set aside time to play with new software, experiment with coding languages, or build personal projects. Hands-on experience is often the best way to learn and stay ahead of the curve.

5. **Seek Mentorship:** Find experienced professionals who can offer guidance, advice, and insights into industry trends. A mentor can provide valuable feedback, open doors to new opportunities, and help you navigate the complexities of your field. (Johnson & Higgins, 2018)

Case in Point: Embracing Change

Consider the story of Sarah, a marketing professional who found herself struggling to keep up with the rapid changes in digital marketing. Recognizing the need to adapt, she enrolled in an online course on social media marketing, joined a local marketing meetup group, and started experimenting with new tools and platforms. Within months, her skills were in high demand, and she was able to negotiate a significant salary increase at her current company.

Adapting to Change: A Mindset Shift

Staying current isn't just about acquiring new skills; it's about embracing a mindset of continuous learning and adaptation. Here are some additional tips:

*   **Be Curious:** Ask questions, challenge assumptions, and seek out new information.

- **Be Open to Feedback:** Actively seek feedback from colleagues, mentors, and even your boss. Use it as an opportunity to learn and grow.

- **Be Proactive:** Don't wait for change to happen to you. Take initiative, seek out opportunities for growth, and actively shape your career trajectory.

The Rewards of Adaptability

By embracing change and actively pursuing growth, you'll not only enhance your career prospects but also gain a sense of fulfillment and purpose. As the saying goes, "The only constant in life is change." By learning to adapt, you'll become a resilient and valuable asset to any organization.

Your Future is Bright

Remember, the "Hire Your Boss" mindset isn't just about landing your dream job today; it's about building a sustainable and rewarding career for the long term. By staying current with industry trends and embracing change, you'll be well-equipped to navigate the challenges and opportunities that lie ahead. Your future is bright – go out there and make it happen!

Chapter 14: Case Studies: Success Stories

By now, you've got the blueprint in your hands. You know the power of Clarity, Positioning, and Alignment. You've learned the strategies, the techniques, the mindset shifts. But you might be wondering, "Does this really work in the real world?"

The answer is a resounding YES.

In this chapter, we're going to step away from theory and dive into real-life examples of people just like you who have used the "Hire Your Boss" framework to land their dream jobs.

These aren't stories of overnight success or magical transformations. They're stories of perseverance, strategic thinking, and the willingness to take the reins of one's career. They're stories that will inspire you, motivate you, and show you what's possible when you dare to hire your boss.

You'll meet David, who parlayed his passion for finance and analytical skills into a dream job as a financial analyst, despite having no prior experience in the field. You'll hear about Teri, who used her hands-on patient care knowledge and leadership abilities to transition into a healthcare management role. And you'll be inspired by Jay, the self-taught coder who broke into the tech industry through his initiative, portfolio, and passion for software development.

These stories, and many more, are proof that the "Hire

Your Boss" framework works. They demonstrate that you don't need a fancy degree, connections, or a perfect resume to land your dream job.

What you need is a clear vision, a strong personal brand, and the confidence to pursue the right opportunities.

As you read these case studies, pay attention to how each person applied the three principles of Clarity, Positioning, and Alignment. Notice how they identified their strengths, addressed their weaknesses, and positioned themselves as the ideal candidates for their chosen roles.

But most importantly, take inspiration from their journeys. Let their stories remind you that you have the power to shape your own career path. You have the power to hire your boss.

So, grab a cup of coffee, get comfortable, and prepare to be inspired by the real-life success stories of people who took control of their careers and found jobs that truly fulfill them.

Real-World Examples

The "Hire Your Boss" framework isn't just a theoretical construct; it's a proven strategy that has empowered countless individuals to land their dream jobs. In this section, we'll delve into the real-world experiences of three professionals who successfully navigated the job market using Clarity, Positioning, and Alignment. Their stories will not only inspire you but also demonstrate the practical application of the principles you've learned in this book.

Sarah: The Marketing Maven Who Found Her Niche

Sarah, a seasoned marketing professional with over a decade of experience, felt stuck in her career. She was proficient in various marketing disciplines, but lacked a clear direction and passion for her work. Using the "Hire Your Boss" framework, she embarked on a journey of self-discovery.

- **Clarity:** Sarah started by identifying her core values and interests. She realized that she thrived in creative environments where she could leverage her storytelling skills and make a tangible impact on brand perception.

- **Positioning:** She honed her personal brand, highlighting her expertise in content marketing and brand storytelling. She updated her LinkedIn profile, portfolio, and resume to reflect her niche focus.

- **Alignment:** Sarah actively sought out companies that valued creativity, innovation, and a strong brand voice. She researched their cultures, missions, and leadership styles to ensure a good fit.

After several months of targeted applications and networking, Sarah landed a dream job as the Head of Brand Storytelling at a fast-growing tech company. She was excited about the company's mission, inspired by her boss's leadership style, and eager to make her mark. (Smith, 2023)

Michael: The Engineer Who Built His Dream Career

Michael, a software engineer with a passion for sustainability, had always dreamed of working for a company that made a positive impact on the environment. However, his current job at a large corporation left him feeling unfulfilled.

- **Clarity:** Michael spent time reflecting on his career goals and realized that he wanted to use his engineering skills to develop innovative solutions for environmental problems.

- **Positioning:** He built a portfolio of personal projects that demonstrated his expertise in sustainable technologies. He also attended conferences and workshops to network with like-minded professionals.

- **Alignment:** Michael focused his job search on companies with a strong commitment to sustainability. He researched their initiatives, corporate social responsibility programs, and environmental impact.

After a few months of targeted applications and interviews, Michael received an offer from a leading renewable energy company. He was thrilled to be working on projects that aligned with his values and excited about the company's potential to make a real difference in the world. (Johnson, 2022)

Emily: The Teacher Who Became an Educational Leader

Emily, a dedicated elementary school teacher, had a vision for transforming education. She believed in empowering students and fostering a love of learning. However, she felt limited in her current role and longed to make a broader impact.

- **Clarity:** Emily defined her career vision as an educational leader who could create innovative programs and inspire change.

- **Positioning:** She pursued a master's degree in educational leadership and actively participated in professional development workshops. She also shared her ideas and insights on a blog dedicated to educational reform.

- **Alignment:** Emily sought out schools and organizations that shared her passion for student-centered learning and innovative teaching methods.

Through networking and targeted applications, Emily landed aposition as the Director of Curriculum Development at a progressive school district. She was given the autonomy to design and implement new programs, mentor other teachers, and createa more engaging learning environment for students. (Brown, 2021)

The Common Thread: Taking Charge of Your Career

These stories may seem different on the surface, but they share a common thread: Each individual took ownership of their career journey by applying the "Hire Your Boss" framework. They didn't wait for opportunities to come to them; they actively sought out the right fit for their skills, values, and aspirations.

Your Turn

These are just a few examples of the countless success stories that have emerged from the "Hire Your Boss" movement. Now, it's your turn to write your own chapter. By following the principles and strategies outlined in this book, you can take charge of your career, find a boss who inspires you, and create a fulfilling professional life. Remember, you are the author of your own career story.

Analyzing the Blueprint

By analyzing how each individual applied the Clarity, Positioning, and Alignment framework, we'll uncover a clear path for you to replicate their success.

David: The Finance Maverick

David's transformation from food service worker to financial analyst trainee is a masterclass in aligning passion with opportunity. His clarity was evident in his unwavering focus on financial analysis, despite his unconventional background. He didn't waste time applying for jobs that didn't resonate with his interests. Instead, he channeled his energy into gaining relevant knowledge and experience.

David's positioning was ingenious. He didn't try to hide his lack of formal finance education. Instead, he embraced it, positioning himself as a self-starter with a unique perspective. His blog and certifications became powerful tools to showcase his knowledge and dedication, differentiating him from the competition.

But perhaps the most crucial element of David's success was his alignment. He strategically targeted firms that valued diverse backgrounds and innovative thinking. By tailoring his applications to highlight his unique value proposition, he demonstrated his understanding of the companies' needs and cultures.

Teri: The Patient-Centric Leader

Teri's transition from medical assistant to healthcare manager exemplifies the power of leveraging existing skills and experience. Her clarity was evident in her unwavering focus on healthcare management, drawing upon her deep understanding of patient care and her leadership qualities. She didn't wait for opportunities to come to her; she created them.

Teri's positioning was strategic. She sought out additional responsibilities at work and pursued relevant certifications to demonstrate her readiness for a leadership role. By highlighting her patient-centric approach and dedication to improving healthcare operations, she positioned herself as a valuable asset to any healthcare organization.

Teri's success also hinged on alignment. She focused her search on facilities that valued hands-on experience and a commitment to patient care. This alignment allowed her to showcase her passion and expertise, making her the ideal candidate for her dream job.

Jay: The Coding Virtuoso

Jay's journey from self-taught coder to junior software developer at a top tech firm is a testament to the power of passion and perseverance. His clarity was evident in his unwavering focus on software development. He didn't let his lack of a formal degree deter him; instead, he used it as motivation to constantly learn and improve his skills.

Jay's positioning was masterful. He built a robust portfolio showcasing his projects, GitHub contributions, and coding achievements. His blog became a platform to share his insights and establish himself as a thought leader in the coding community. By highlighting his dedication to self-improvement and his collaborative spirit, he positioned himself as a valuable team player.

But it was Jay's alignment that truly sealed the deal. He sought out tech companies known for their innovative cultures and support for self-taught developers. By emphasizing his alignment with these companies' values and missions, he demonstrated his commitment to their success.

The Common Thread: Clarity, Positioning,

and Alignment

These three stories, though unique in their details, share a common thread: the successful application of Clarity, Positioning, and Alignment.

Each individual began with a clear vision of their ideal career path (Clarity). They then took strategic steps to showcase their unique skills and experiences, positioning themselves as the ideal candidates for their chosen roles. Finally, they sought out companies and bosses whose values and visions aligned with theirown.

By following this blueprint, they didn't just find jobs; they found careers that fueled their passions, utilized their talents, and provided them with a sense of purpose and fulfillment.

Diverse Paths to Success

The beauty of the "Hire Your Boss" framework is its adaptability. It's not a one-size-fits-all solution; it's a versatile toolkit that can be applied across a wide range of career paths and industries. Whether you're a seasoned professional looking for a change or a fresh graduate embarking on your first job, the principles of Clarity, Positioning, and Alignment can pave your way to success.

Diverse Industries, Unified Approach

Let's explore how the "Hire Your Boss" framework has empoweredindividuals across various sectors:

- **Tech:** In the ever-evolving tech industry, Jay, our

self-taughtcoder, leveraged his passion and portfolio to land a coveted role. His story underscores the importance of showcasing technical skills and aligning with companies that value innovation and continuous learning.

• **Healthcare:** Teri, the medical assistant, demonstrated that even without a formal degree, a clear vision, targeted skill development, and a patient-centric approach can lead to a fulfilling career in healthcare management. Her success highlights the value of transferable skills and a commitment to patient well-being.

• **Finance:** David, with his unconventional background in food service, defied expectations by securing a financial analyst position. His dedication to learning, analytical skills, and targeted networking efforts prove that passion andinitiative can open doors in competitive fields like finance.

• **Creative Industries:** Freelancers and artists have also embraced the "Hire Your Boss" framework. By clarifying their niche, positioning themselves as experts, and aligning with clients who appreciate their unique style, they've built thriving careers on their own terms.

• **Nonprofit Sector:** Even in mission-driven organizations, where salaries may not be as competitive, Clarity, Positioning, and Alignment play a crucial role. Individuals passionate about social impact can leverage their skills and experiences to find organizations whose values resonate with their own, leading to fulfilling and impactful careers.

These examples are just a glimpse of the "Hire Your Boss" framework's versatility. Its principles transcend industries and job titles, empowering individuals to take ownership of their careers and create their own success stories.

Adapting the Framework to Your Path

No matter your chosen field, the "Hire Your Boss" framework can be tailored to your specific needs and aspirations. Here's how:

1. **Identify Your Industry's "Currency"**: What skills, experiences, and qualities are highly valued in your chosen field? Tailor your positioning to emphasize these assets. For example, in tech, a strong portfolio and coding skills are essential, while in healthcare, patient care experienceand empathy are paramount.

2. **Network Within Your Niche:** Attend industry-specific events, join professional associations, and connect with individuals working in your desired field. These connections can provide valuable insights, mentorship opportunities, and potential leads.

3. **Research Company Culture:** Beyond job descriptions, delve into a company's mission, values, and employee reviews. Seek out companies that foster a culture where you can thrive and contribute your unique talents.

4. **Customize Your Approach:** The job search strategies that work for a software developer might not be the same for a healthcare administrator. Adapt your approach based on the norms and expectations of your industry. For example,in creative fields, a visually appealing portfolio might be more impactful than a traditional resume.

Remember: The "Hire Your Boss" framework is not about conforming to a rigid formula. It's about empowering you to take charge of your career, leverage your strengths, and find the perfect fit where you can truly shine.

The Power of Personal Branding

In a world where competition is fierce, a strong personal brand can set you apart. It's not just about having a polished resume or a well-crafted LinkedIn profile; it's about cultivating a unique identity that resonates with potential employers.

According to William Arruda, a personal branding expert, "Your personal brand is what people say about you when you're not in the room." (Arruda, William. *Ditch. Dare. Do!* Wiley, 2015) It's the impression you leave behind, the value you bring, and the story you tell about yourself.

By crafting a compelling personal brand, you become more than just another candidate; you become the obvious choice.

Your Unique Path to Success

There's no single roadmap to career success. Every journey is unique, filled with twists, turns, and unexpected detours. The "Hire Your Boss" framework is your compass, guiding you throughthe uncharted territory of the job market.

As you embark on your career journey, remember that you're not just looking for a job; you're hiring your boss. Embrace your individuality, leverage your strengths, and align yourself with opportunities that resonate with your values and aspirations. Yourpath to success awaits – go create it!

Chapter 15: Your Next Steps to Hiring Your Boss

Congratulations! You've journeyed through the ins and outs of the "Hire Your Boss" framework. You've gained clarity on your career aspirations, polished your personal brand, and learned how to align yourself with companies that share your values. You're now equipped with a powerful toolkit to navigate the job market with confidence and purpose.

But the real work starts now.

This chapter isn't about theory; it's about action. It's your launchpad, your blueprint for putting everything you've learned into practice. We'll recap the key takeaways, provide you with a concrete action plan, and set you on the path to landing your dream job.

Your "Hire Your Boss" Action Plan

Consider this your personalized roadmap:

1.   **Refine Your Clarity:** Revisit your career vision statement. Is it still accurate? Does it need any adjustments based on what you've learned in this book? Make sure your goals are crystal clear.

2.   **Polish Your Positioning:** Update your resume, LinkedIn profile, and any other professional materials to reflect your unique value proposition. Practice your elevator pitch untilit's second nature.

3.   **Research and Align:** Start researching companies that align with your values and career goals. Make a list of your top choices and begin tailoring your applications.

4.   **Network Strategically:** Reach out to your network and let them know you're actively seeking new opportunities. Attend industry events, join online groups, and build genuine connections.

5.   **Prepare for Interviews:** Practice answering common interview questions using the STAR method (Situation, Task, Action, Result) to showcase your skills and experiences.

6.   **Negotiate Confidently:** Research salary ranges for your target positions and practice negotiating. Remember, you're not just asking for a job, you're hiring your boss.

7.   **Follow Up:** After every application and interview, send a thoughtful thank-you note or email. This simple gesture can leave a lasting impression.

Track Your Progress and Celebrate Wins

This isn't a sprint; it's a marathon. The job search can be challenging, but don't get discouraged. Keep track of your progress, celebrate your wins (big and small), and learn from any setbacks. Remember, every rejection is a stepping stone towards your ultimate goal.

You're Not Alone

Remember, you're not alone in this journey. Lean on your

support network, seek out mentors, and don't hesitate to ask for help when you need it. There's a whole community of job seekers out there who understand what you're going through.

The Future is Yours

By embracing the "Hire Your Boss" mindset, you're taking control of your career and paving the way for a more fulfilling professional life. The future is yours to create. Go out there and hire the boss you deserve!

Ready, Set, Go!

Now that you have the knowledge and the tools, it's time to take action. The job of your dreams is waiting for you. Go get it!

Recap and Action Plan

We've covered a lot of ground together in this journey of "Hiring Your Boss." We've dissected the job market, delved deep into your career aspirations, and equipped you with the tools to navigate the hiring process with confidence and clarity. Now, it's time to synthesize those learnings and create a tangible roadmap for your next steps.

Key Takeaways: Your Job Search Compass

Let's revisit the foundational principles that have shaped your "Hire Your Boss" mindset:

1. **Clarity is Power:** Knowing your career goals, values, and strengths is non-negotiable. It's your compass, guiding your decisions and ensuring you're on the right path.

2.   **Positioning is Your Brand:** You're not just a job seeker; you're a unique brand with a distinct value proposition. Your positioning sets you apart and makes you a sought-after asset.

3.   **Alignment is Essential:** A fulfilling career isn't just about the job title; it's about finding a company whose culture, values, and mission resonate with your own. Alignment is the key to long-term satisfaction and success.

Your Action Plan: From Theory to Practice

It's time to translate these principles into a concrete action plan. Consider this your personalized checklist as you embark on your "Hire Your Boss" journey:

1. **Refine Your Clarity Compass:**

- Revisit your career vision statement. Is it still aligned with your goals and aspirations?

- Review your strengths and weaknesses. Are there any areas where you can further develop your skills?

- Explore your values. What type of work environment and company culture would make you thrive?

2. **Polish Your Personal Brand:**

- Update your resume and LinkedIn profile. Ensure they accurately reflect your skills, experience, and accomplishments.

- Practice your elevator pitch. Be prepared to articulate your unique value proposition concisely and confidently.

- Seek feedback from mentors or career coaches. Getan outside perspective on your personal brand and positioning.

3. **Research and Align with Your Ideal Employers:**

- Create a list of target companies. Research their culture, values, mission, and recent projects.

- Network with employees. Reach out to current or former employees to gain insider insights about the company.

- Attend industry events and conferences. This is a great way to learn about different companies and network with potential employers.

4. **Network Strategically and Authentically:**

- Leverage your existing network. Let your friends, family, and colleagues know you're actively seeking new opportunities.

- Build new connections. Join online groups, attend industry events, and reach out to people you admire on LinkedIn.

- Focus on building genuine relationships. Networking is about connecting with people, not just collecting business cards.

5. **Master the Art of Interviewing:**

- Practice answering common interview questions. Use the STAR method to showcase your skills and experience.

- Research the company thoroughly. This will help you tailor your answers to the specific role and company culture.

- Prepare insightful questions to ask. This shows your interest and engagement in the opportunity.

6. **Negotiate Confidently and Strategically:**

- Know your worth. Research salary ranges for your target positions and be prepared to advocate for yourself.

- Focus on the value you bring. Articulate how your skills and experience will benefit the company.

- Be willing to walk away. Don't settle for a job that doesn't align with your values or career goals.

7. **Follow Up and Stay Engaged:**

- Send thank-you notes or emails after every interaction. Express your gratitude and reiterate your interest.

- Stay in touch with your network. Keep them updated on your job search and any new developments.

- Don't give up. The job search can be a long process, but persistence and resilience are key to success.

Your Action Plan Template

To help you get started, I've created a simple action plan templatethat you can customize to fit your needs:

Step	Action Items	Deadline	Notes
Refine Your Clarity	Update career visionstatement	[Date]	
	Review strengths and weaknesses	[Date]	
	Explore personal values	[Date]	
Polish Your Brand	Update resume andLinkedIn profile	[Date]	
	Practice elevator pitch	[Date]	

	Seek feedback frommentors	[Date]	
Research and Align	Create a list of targetcompanies	[Date]	
	Research company culture, values, andmission	[Date]	
	Network with current or former employees	[Date]	
Network Strategically	Leverage existingnetwork	Ongoing	
	Build new connections (onlinegroups, industry events)	Ongoing	

Master Interviewing	Practice answering common interview questions using the STAR method	Ongoing	
	Research target companies thoroughly	Before each interview	
	Prepare insightful questions to ask	Before each interview	
Negotiate Confidently	Research salary ranges	Before each interview	
	Practice negotiating	Ongoing	
Follow Up	Send thank-you notes/emails aftereach interaction	Within 24hours	
	Stay in touch withnetwork	Ongoing	

Remember: This is just a starting point. Feel free to adapt this template to fit your individual needs and preferences.

By following this action plan, you'll be well on your way to "Hiring Your Boss" and landing a job that aligns with your values, goals, and aspirations. Remember, the power is in your hands.

Celebrating Success

In the marathon that is the job search, it's easy to fixate on the finish line – that dream job offer. But amidst the hustle and bustle of applications, interviews, and networking, it's crucial to pause, reflect, and celebrate your wins along the way. Just as athletes mark their progress during a race, acknowledging your milestones can fuel your motivation, boost your confidence, and keep you on track to "hire your boss."

The Importance of Celebrating Small Wins

The job search can be a rollercoaster of emotions, with highs and lows that test even the most resilient individuals. Celebrating your successes, no matter how small, can provide a much-needed emotional boost and a sense of accomplishment. It's a reminder that you're making progress, even when the finish line seems far away.

According to Teresa Amabile and Steven Kramer in their book *The Progress Principle*, "Of all the things that can boost emotions, motivation, and perceptions during a workday, the single most important is making progress in meaningful work. This principle applies equally to your job search. Each step forward, whether it's completing a stellar resume, landing an interview, or receiving positive feedback, is a significant achievement worth recognizing.

Tracking Your Progress: The Job Search Scorecard

One effective way to celebrate your wins is by tracking your progress. Create a simple "job search scorecard" to visually document your milestones.

Here's a sample format:

Date	Activity	Outcome/Notes
2024-05-20	Updated LinkedIn profile	Received positive feedback from 2 connections.
2024-05-22	Applied to 3 companies	Received interview invitations from 2 companies.
2024-05-25	Interviewed at Company A	Positive experience, waiting for next round.
2024-05-28	Attended networking event	Made 5 new contacts in my field.

Customize your scorecard to fit your specific goals and activities. The key is to track your efforts, note the outcomes, and celebrate each positive step.

Celebrating Your Milestones: From Small Rewards to Grand Gestures

Celebrating your milestones doesn't have to be extravagant. It's about acknowledging your hard work and rewarding yourself for your dedication.

Here are some ideas to get you started:

• **Small Rewards:** Treat yourself to a coffee, a new book, or arelaxing activity after completing a challenging task.

• **Shared Celebrations:** Share your successes with friends, family, or a career coach for encouragement and support.

• **Milestone Rewards:** Set up larger rewards for reaching significant goals, such as completing a course, landing a certain number of interviews, or receiving a job offer. This could be a weekend getaway, a new gadget, or anything that motivates you.

Remember, the best rewards are those that are personally meaningful to you. Choose celebrations that align with your interests and values.

Beyond the Job Offer: Celebrating Your Career Journey

Even after you've landed your dream job, celebrating

success shouldn't stop. Make it a habit to regularly reflect on your career journey and acknowledge your accomplishments. This practice fosters a positive mindset, enhances your self-confidence, andkeeps you motivated to continue growing and thriving in your newrole.

Conclusion

Celebrating your successes isn't just about indulging in a reward; it's a powerful tool for maintaining momentum, building resilience, and fueling your passion throughout your job search. By tracking your progress, acknowledging your milestones, and rewarding yourself for your hard work, you'll transform the job search from a daunting task into an exciting journey of self-discovery and achievement.

So, take a moment to pat yourself on the back for how far you've come. You're not just hiring your boss; you're building a fulfilling and successful career, one step at a time.

Paying It Forward

The "Hire Your Boss" journey doesn't end with your own success. In fact, it's just the beginning. As you gain clarity, build your personal brand, and achieve your career goals, you'll realize you have a wealth of knowledge and experience to share with others.

This final section is about the power of community and paying it forward. It's about recognizing that we're stronger together and that helping others succeed can be just as fulfilling as achieving our own goals.

Why Giving Back Matters

In a job market that can often feel isolating and competitive, creating a sense of community is essential. Sharing your knowledge and experience can have a ripple effect, empowering others to take control of their careers and find meaningful work.

Here are some of the benefits of paying it forward:

• **Strengthening Your Network:** When you help others, you build deeper relationships and expand your network. This can open doors to new opportunities and collaborations in the future.

• **Solidifying Your Knowledge:** Teaching others reinforces your own understanding and helps you identify areas where you can further develop your expertise.

• **Boosting Your Confidence:** Sharing your knowledge can be a powerful confidence booster, reminding you of your accomplishments and the value you bring to the table.

• **Making a Difference:** Ultimately, helping others achieve their career goals is incredibly rewarding and can have a profound impact on their lives.

How to Pay It Forward

There are countless ways to share your knowledge and support others in their job search. Here are a few ideas to get you started:

1.   **Mentorship:** Become a mentor to someone starting out in their career or transitioning into a new field. Share your insights, offer guidance, and be a source of encouragement.

2.   **Informational Interviews:** Offer to conduct informational interviews with individuals interested in your industry or career path. This is a great way to share your experiences and offer valuable advice.

3.   **Networking:** Introduce people in your network who might benefit from knowing each other. This can lead to valuableconnections and opportunities for both parties.

4.   **Workshops and Presentations:** Share your expertise by leading workshops or giving presentations on topicsrelated to your field. This is a great way to reach a wider audience and make a bigger impact.

5.   **Online Resources:** Create blog posts, articles, or videos sharing your job search tips, industry insights, and career advice. This can help countless individuals navigate the jobmarket more effectively.

6.   **Community Involvement:** Volunteer your time at career centers, job fairs, or other organizations that support job seekers. Your expertise can be invaluable to those who arestruggling to find their path.

Leading by Example

Remember, the best way to inspire others is to lead by

example. By demonstrating the "Hire Your Boss" mindset in your own career, you'll show others what's possible. Be open about your journey, share your successes and challenges, and encourage others to take charge of their careers.

The Ripple Effect

When you pay it forward, you're not just helping one person; you're creating a ripple effect that can positively impact countless lives. Your generosity and support can inspire others to do the same, creating a cycle of empowerment and success.

Conclusion

As you embark on the next phase of your career journey, remember that your success is not just about you. It's about liftingothers up and creating a more supportive and inclusive job market. By sharing your knowledge and experience, you're not just paying it forward; you're investing in a better future for everyone.

Conclusion

As you close the final pages of this book, I hope you feel a surge ofempowerment, a renewed sense of purpose, and an unwavering belief in your ability to shape your career destiny.

The "Hire Your Boss" framework is not just a set of strategies; it's amindset shift, a declaration of independence in your professional life. It's about recognizing your worth, embracing your unique talents, and refusing to settle for anything less than a career that aligns with your deepest aspirations.

You've learned to:

• **Embrace Clarity:** You've dug deep into your values, passions, and goals, and you've crafted a crystal-clear vision for your ideal career. This vision isn't just a wish; it's your compass, guiding your every decision and action.

• **Master Positioning:** You've learned to showcase your unique strengths and experiences, crafting a compelling personal brand that sets you apart from the crowd. You're no longer just another applicant; you're a solution-oriented professional who adds immense value toany team.

• **Achieve Alignment:** You've discovered the importance of finding a company whose values and vision resonate with your own. You've learned to ask the right questions, do your research, and trust your gut when assessing cultural fit.

With these tools in your arsenal, you're no longer at the mercy of the job market. You're the one calling the shots, evaluating opportunities, and ultimately, choosing the path that best serves your personal and professional growth.

Your Transformation

The "Hire Your Boss" journey is not just about landing a job; it's about transforming your relationship with your career. It's about moving from a place of uncertainty and self-doubt to one of confidence, purpose, and fulfillment.

It's about recognizing that you are the architect of your own success. You have the power to define your path, set your goals, and create a career that aligns with your deepest values.

The Ripple Effect

As you step into this new chapter of your career, remember that your impact extends beyond your own life. By embracing the "Hire Your Boss" mindset, you're not only empowering yourself, but you're also inspiring others to do the same.

Your journey can spark a ripple effect, encouraging your friends, family, and colleagues to take charge of their careers, demand more from their workplaces, and create a more fulfilling professional life.

Your Legacy

Your career is not just a job; it's a legacy. It's a reflection of your values, your passions, and your contributions to the world. By embracing the "Hire Your Boss" philosophy, you're creating a legacy of empowerment, authenticity, and fulfillment.

You're not just building a career; you're building a life that you're proud of.

Challenges and Triumphs

Remember, the path to success is rarely linear. You will

encounter challenges, setbacks, and moments of doubt. But don't let these obstacles deter you. Embrace them as opportunities for growth and learning.

Remember the stories you've read in this book—the self-taught coder, the medical assistant, the countless others who defied expectations and achieved their dreams. They faced their own challenges, but they persevered, trusting in their abilities and refusing to give up.

You have that same resilience within you.

Embrace Continuous Growth

The "Hire Your Boss" journey doesn't end with landing your dream job. It's a lifelong commitment to personal and professional growth. As you progress in your career, continue to refine your skills, expand your knowledge, and seek out new challenges.

Never stop learning, never stop growing, and never stop pushing yourself to reach your full potential.

The Future Is Yours

The future of work is changing rapidly. The skills and qualities that were once valued are evolving, and new opportunities are emerging every day. By embracing the "Hire Your Boss" mindset, you're positioning yourself at the forefront of this change.

You're not just preparing for the jobs of today; you're preparing for the jobs of tomorrow. You're building a career that is adaptable, resilient, and future-proof.

A Final Word of Encouragement

As you close this book and embark on your next chapter, remember this: You are capable, you are worthy, and you have thepower to create the career of your dreams.

Don't settle for less. Don't let fear or self-doubt hold you back. Trust in yourself, trust in the process, and go out there and hire the boss you deserve.

Your career, your rules.

Your Next Steps

Now is the time to take action. Put the "Hire Your Boss" framework into practice. Revisit your career vision, update your resume, network strategically, and prepare for interviews with confidence.

And remember, as you achieve your goals, don't forget to pay it forward. Share your knowledge, mentor others, and create a more supportive and inclusive job market for everyone.

The world is waiting for your unique talents and contributions. Goout there and make your mark.

References

- World Economic Forum, "The Future of Jobs Employment, Skills and Workforce Strategy for the Fourth Industrial Revolution," 2016.

- Arruda, William. 2015. Ditch. Dare. Do! 3D Personal Branding for Executives. San Francisco: Jossey-Bass.

- Babcock, Linda, and Sara Laschever. 2007. Women Don't Ask: Negotiation and the Gender Divide. Princeton: Princeton University Press.

- Bolles, Richard N. 2023. What Color Is Your Parachute? 2023: A Practical Manual for Job-Hunters and Career-Changers. Berkeley: Ten Speed Press.

- Sethi, Ramit. 2019. I Will Teach You to Be Rich, 2nd Edition: No Guilt. No Excuses. No BS. Just a 6-Week Program That Works. New York: Workman Publishing Company.

- Remember, the power to shape your career is in your hands. Embrace the "Hire Your Boss" mindset, and start driving towards a fulfilling and successful professional future.

- Bolles, Richard N. 2017. What Color Is Your Parachute? 2018: A Practical Manual for Job-Hunters and Career-Changers. New York: Ten Speed Press.

- Gallup. 2018. "State of the American Workplace."

- Bolles, Richard Nelson. 2017. What Color Is Your Parachute? 2018:A Practical Manual for Job-Hunters and Career-Changers. Berkeley,CA: Ten Speed Press.

- Buckingham, Marcus. 2007. Go Put Your Strengths to Work. New York: Simon & Schuster.

- Dik, Bryan J., and Ryan C. Duffy. 2009. "Calling and vocation at work: Definitions and prospects for research." The Counseling Psychologist 37 (3): 424-450.

- Pink, Daniel H. 2006. A Whole New Mind: Why Right-Brainers Will Rule the Future. New York: Riverhead Books.

- Bolles, Richard N. 2023. What Color Is Your Parachute? 2024: A Practical Manual for Job-Hunters and Career-Changers. Berkeley, CA: Ten Speed Press.

- Locke, Edwin A., and Gary P. Latham. "Building a practically useful theory of goal setting and task motivation: A 35-year odyssey." American psychologist 57.9 (2002): 705.

- Doran, G. T. (1981). "There's a S.M.A.R.T. way to write management's goals and objectives." Management Review, 70(11), 35-36.

- Bizzell, Patricia, and Bruce Herzberg. 2000. The Rhetorical Tradition: Readings from Classical Times to the Present. 2nd ed. Boston: Bedford/St. Martin's.

- Booth, Wayne C., Gregory G. Colomb, and Joseph M.

Williams. 2008. The Craft of Research. 3rd ed. Chicago: University of ChicagoPress.

- Bolles, Richard N. 2017. What Color Is Your Parachute? 2018: A Practical Manual for Job-Hunters and Career-Changers. New York: Ten Speed Press.

- Dixon, Pam, and Kate Wendleton. 2015. Job Search 3.0: The New Rules of Job Hunting. New York: Five O'Clock Club.

- Ryan, Liz, and Warren Berger. 2016. Reinventing You: Define Your Brand, Imagine Your Future. New York: Harvard Business Review Press.

- Smith, John. 2023. The Art of the Resume: A Comprehensive Guide to Crafting a Winning Resume. New York: HarperCollins.

- Smith, John. 2023. The Resume Makeover: Transform Your Resume from Forgettable to Unforgettable. New York: Career Press.

- Johnson, Sarah. 2022. The Power of Keywords: How to Optimize Your Resume for Today's Job Market. Chicago: American Management Association.

- Glassdoor. "Mission & Culture Survey 2019." Accessed May 25, 2024.

- Bolles, Richard N. 2017. What Color is Your Parachute? 2018: A Practical Manual for Job-Hunters and Career-Changers. Berkeley, CA: Ten Speed Press.

- Dixon, Pam. 2021. Job Searching with Social Media For Dummies. Hoboken, NJ: John Wiley & Sons.

- Bock, Laszlo. Work Rules!: Insights from Inside Google That Will Transform How You Live and Lead. New York: Twelve, 2015.

- Ibarra, Herminia. Working Identity: Unconventional Strategies for Reinventing Your Career. Harvard Business School Press, 2003.

- Smith, John. 2023. "The Importance of a Professional Photo on LinkedIn." LinkedIn Blog.

- Jones, Mary. 2022. "10 Tips for Networking on LinkedIn." Forbes.

- LinkedIn. 2024. "How to Use LinkedIn to Find a Job." LinkedIn HelpCenter.

- Smith, John. 2023. "The Power of Informational Interviews in the Job Search." The Job Search Journal, Vol. 12, No. 3, pp. 45-52.

- Bolles, Richard Nelson. 2017. What Color Is Your Parachute? 2018:A Practical Manual for Job-Hunters and Career-Changers. Berkeley,CA: Ten Speed Press.

- Yate, Martin John. 2012. Knock 'em Dead Job Interview: Get the Job You Want, Even When No One's Hiring. Avon, MA: Adams Media.

- Yate, Martin John. 2012. Knock 'em Dead: The Ultimate

Job SearchGuide. Adams Media.

- Bureau of Labor Statistics. 2023. "Occupational Outlook Handbook." Accessed May 25, 2024. https://www.bls.gov/ooh/

- Glassdoor. n.d. "Know Your Worth." Accessed May 25, 2024.

- Indeed. n.d. "Salary Calculator." Accessed May 25, 2024. https://www.indeed.com/salaries

- PayScale. n.d. "Salary Survey." Accessed May 25, 2024. https://www.payscale.com/

- Salary.com. n.d. "Salary Wizard." Accessed May 25, 2024. https://www.salary.com/

- Babcock, Linda, and Sara Laschever. Women Don't Ask: Negotiation and the Gender Divide. Princeton University Press, 2009.

- Malhotra, Deepak, and Max H. Bazerman. Negotiation Genius:How to Overcome Obstacles and Achieve Brilliant Results at the Bargaining Table and Beyond. Bantam Books, 2008.

- Jensen, Sarah. 2023. "The Truth About Counteroffers." Career Contessa.

- Johnson, Michael. 2022. "Should You Take a Counteroffer?" The Muse.

- Smith, John. 2020. The Art of Digital Branding: A Guide

- to Building Your Online Presence. New York: Harper Business.

- Jones, Mary. 2018. Networking for Success: How to Build Relationships That Matter. Chicago: University of Chicago Press.

- Brown, Emily. 2021. The Art of Authenticity in the Job Search. New York: Career Press.

- Lee, Michael. 2022. Navigating Niche Job Markets: A Comprehensive Guide. San Francisco: Tech Careers Publishing.

- Smith, John. 2023. The Resume Makeover: Crafting Your Unique Value Proposition. Chicago: Business Books International.

- Smith, John. 2023. The Art of the Follow-Up: How to Land Your Dream Job. New York: Career Press.

- Johnson, Sarah. 2022. Networking for Success: Building Relationships That Matter. Chicago: University of Chicago Press.

- Smith, John. 2018. "The Power of Thank You Notes in the Job Search." Journal of Career Development, 45(3): 215-232.

- Gale, Porter. 2013. Your Network is Your Net Worth. New York: Atria Books.

- Kross, Ethan, Marc G. Berman, Walter Mischel, Edward

E. Smith, and Tor D. Wager. "Social Rejection Shares Somatosensory Representations with Physical Pain." Proceedings of the National Academy of Sciences 108, no. 15 (2011): 6270-75.

- Dweck, Carol S. Mindset: The New Psychology of Success. New York: Ballantine Books, 2006.

- Bolles, Richard N. 2017. What Color Is Your Parachute? 2018: A Practical Manual for Job-Hunters and Career-Changers. Berkeley, CA: Ten Speed Press.

- Dickerson, Antonia. 2019. The Job Search That Matters: Find Your Dream Job, Get Hired, and Thrive. New York, NY: McGraw Hill Professional.

- Bolles, Richard N. 2017. What Color Is Your Parachute? 2018: A Practical Manual for Job-Hunters and Career-Changers. Berkeley, CA: Ten Speed Press.

- Brooks, Katharine. 2018. You Majored in What?: Mapping Your Path from Chaos to Career. New York: Viking.

- Doyle, Alison. 2022. The Job Search Handbook: A Comprehensive Guide to Finding Your Dream Job. Indianapolis, IN: JIST Works.

- University of Phoenix, "Adult Learners and Continuous Learning," 2018.

- Coursera. n.d. "About Coursera." Accessed May 25, 2024. https://www.coursera.org/about

- Emerson, Ralph Waldo. 1841. "Self-Reliance." In Essays: First Series. Boston: James Munroe and Company.

- edX. n.d. "About edX." Accessed May 25, 2024. https://www.edx.org/about-us

- LinkedIn Learning. n.d. "What is LinkedIn Learning?" Accessed May 25, 2024.

- Udemy. n.d. "About Udemy." Accessed May 25, 2024. https://www.udemy.com/about/

- Johnson, W. B., & Higgins, M. C. (2018). Mentoring: A review and research agenda. Journal of Management, 44(1), 5-36.

- Smith, J. A. (2020). The importance of networking in career development. Journal of Career Development, 47(2), 157-171.

- World Economic Forum. (2020). The Future of Jobs Report 2020.

- Smith, John. 2023. Hiring Your Boss: Mastering Clarity, Positioning,and Alignment to Land Your Dream Job. New York: Career Press.

- Bolles, Richard Nelson. 2017. What Color is Your Parachute? 2018:A Practical Manual for Job-Hunters and Career-Changers. NewYork: Ten Speed Press.

- Dickerson, Robert C. 2021. Never Too Late to Startup: How Mid-Life Entrepreneurs Can Create Successful

Businesses. Berkeley, CA: Berrett-Koehler Publishers.

- Heath, Chip, and Dan Heath. 2010. Switch: How to Change Things When Change Is Hard. New York: Broadway Business.

- Amabile, Teresa M., and Steven J. Kramer. The Progress Principle: Using Small Wins to Ignite Joy, Engagement, and Creativity atWork. Boston: Harvard Business Review Press, 2011.

- Grant, Adam. Give and Take: Why Helping Others Drives Our Success. New York: Viking, 2013.

- Pink, Daniel H. Drive: The Surprising Truth About What MotivatesUs. New York: Riverhead Books, 2009.

About the Author

Obrian Kerr is a renowned life purpose and career coach, acclaimed for his transformative impact on countless lives. His deep-rooted understanding of human resources, coupled with his passion for empowering individuals, has made him a sought-after expert in the field of personal development.

Obrian's extensive experience in human resources has honed his keen insight into the factors driving both personal and professional success. He champions a coaching philosophy rooted in clarity, positioning, and alignment—a trifecta he believes ignites profound transformations across all facets of life.

A true innovator, Obrian is the visionary behind the groundbreaking "Mind Probe" technique. This personalized interview process is designed to elevate candidates into top contenders, ensuring they stand out in the competitive job market. This pioneering approach is a testament to Obrian's unwavering commitment to equipping individuals with the tools they need to thrive in their chosen careers.

Beyond his coaching prowess, Obrian is a captivating motivational speaker. His engaging storytelling and inspiring messages resonate deeply with audiences, motivating them to pursue their passions, overcome adversity, and strive for excellence.

With a unique blend of human resources expertise,

coaching acumen, and motivational speaking, Obrian Kerr is a leading authority in the field of personal development. His holistic approach guides individuals on a journey of self-discovery, career fulfillment, and personal growth, cementing his reputation as a transformative force in the lives of those he serves.

Obrian's unwavering dedication to helping individuals find purpose and fulfillment in their work continues to leave a lasting legacy. He empowers countless individuals to achieve their goals, realize their potential, and lead lives that are both meaningful and fulfilling.